Shri Guru Gita

108 Sutras for Awakening

Mark Griffin

Hard Light Center of Awakening

Shri Guru Gita © 2008 ~ Mark Griffin
Hard Light Center of Awakening
ISBN 978-0-975902-07-3

All rights reserved. No part of this book may be reproduced in any form or by any means, electronic or mechanical, including photocopying, recording, or by any information storage and retrieval system, without the express written permission from the author.

For more information about the Hard Light Center of Awakening please visit *www.hardlight.org*. The web site provides a complete listing of Mark Griffin's other books and CDs, as well as links to audiobooks, podcasts and PDF books.

The Hard Light Center of Awakening is an organization founded and directed by Mark Griffin as a forum for the study of spirituality and meditation. Mark Griffin is a Meditation Master who is firmly established in the advanced Nirvikalpa Samadhi states — rare strands of consciousness that lead to remarkable perception and spiritual accomplishment.

First Edition: October 2, 2008

Editing, Layout, Typography: PodPublishing

TABLE OF CONTENTS

The Siddha Lineage i

The Structure of the Guru Gita iv

Introduction by Mark Griffin viii

**Shri Guru Gita verses
    for English recitation** 1

**Shri Guru Gita verses
    for Sanskrit recitation** 48
    (with transliteration and English)

Guide to Sanskrit Pronunciation 116

Glossary 120

Additional Resources 151

The Siddha Lineage

Mark Griffin is a Westerner who was born in the 1950's in the Pacific Northwest. His early adult years were spent in the aggressive pursuit of higher knowledge and purpose.

While a young man, Mark's studies in art and music brought him to the San Francisco Bay area. There in 1976 he met his Guru, Baba Muktananda. After years of full-time immersion in the study of meditation, Mark encountered a milestone of extreme spiritual significance – entrance into the advanced state of consciousness known as Nirvikalpa Samadhi. After Muktananda died, Mark continued to study with the great teachers of the Kagyu tradition, Kalu Rinpoche and Chogyam Trungpa, who supported the maturing and stabilizing of his abilities.

In 1989, after attracting several interested students, Mark began to teach meditation. He and his students relocated to Los Angeles and started the Hard Light Center of Awakening, an association dedicated to the art and science of awareness of the Self.

When Mark Griffin met Baba Muktanada he immediately realized that Baba was his Guru, his true teacher. Baba's Guru was the great saint of India, Bhagawan Nityananda of Ganeshpuri. It is with the blessings of these remarkable Siddhas that Mark carries on his inspiring teachings.

An Overview

The recitation of the Guru Gita is one of the practices of the Hard Light Center of Awakening for one simple reason... as Mark Griffin says: "I am teaching you this about the Guru because I believe it's your best chance for Awakening in this lifetime".

The Guru Gita is the core section of 352 sutras in the latter portion of the ancient Indian text known as the Skanda Purana. *Gita* means song, and indeed these sutras are a song in praise of the Guru, and in recognition of the power of contemplating the Guru's nature, especially through the vehicle of the repetition of these verses.

Mark Griffin, the founder of the Hard Light Center of Awakening, has selected 108 of these verses for the use of serious seekers - those who are sincerely interested in spiritual training. This fresh, original translation from the Sanskrit is specifically designed for the contemporary seeker.

These 108 verses focus on the universal nature of the Guru. When the word *Guru* is used here, it is known to be more than an individual person. Rather, it is a universal principle, a catalyst for enlightenment like no other. It is referred to in the text as the *Guru Tattva*, tattva translating as principle.

Let us look for a moment now at the overall structure of the text.

The Structure of Shri Guru Gita

The text uses the classic format of a student asking a teacher a question, with the answer forming the body of the work. In verse 2, the Goddess Parvati cuts right to the heart of the matter and asks Lord Shiva that which her heart most dearly longs to know: "How can I most directly gain realization?"

Shiva begins his answer to Parvati in verse 4 with one phrase that contains the totality of the text: "*The Absolute is the same as the Guru*". Everything unfolds from this core truth. The elaboration of the teaching unfolds from there...

Verses 5 – 71
These verses answer: Who is the Guru? What is his essential nature? What is the method of meditation upon him? What are the benefits of this practice?

Within this large section, there are a few key specific topics to note:

14-16:   The word 'Guru' as mantra

39-47:   The Guru's lotus feet

The Bodhicitta, the inner essence of enlightenment

An Overview

within each person, which abides in the heart-mind is highlighted in verses 46-51. From this perspective, there is no question about whether to visualize the Guru in the heart or in the crown chakra - he is in both, as pointed out by the unity of the heart-mind known as the Bodhicitta:

46-48: Guru meditation in the sahasrar, the crown of the head

49-51: Guru meditation in the heart chakra

64-66: Following the path (margena) of the Guru

Verses 70 - 73
   Now Shiva describes the attributes of a disciple. What is the relationship between the Guru and the disciple? How should the disciple behave? What are the benefits of discipleship?

Verses 73 - 79
   Shiva goes into a more technical explanation of the aspects of realization, defining different levels of experience, and describing the ineffable experience of Unity Consciousness itself. It's interesting to note that Parvati remains an attentive student throughout the discourse that follows. In verse 73 Shiva makes

reference to something she does not understand, and she is quick to interrupt him and ask for an explanation.

Verses 78 – 88
Here begins the description of the nature of a liberated person, and what his life is like based on that awakening.

Verses 89 - 103
Now Shiva begins to discuss the text of the Guru Gita itself, its nature as a mantra, its power in spiritual practices and its ability to enlighten and purify. He also explains how and where it should be recited.

Verse 104 - 108
These verses move into the summary, where Shiva again establishes his authority for expounding this knowledge and admonishing Parvati to follow his teachings.

Join Mark now in singing the praises of this profound Ocean of Consciousness... this force of Awakening – the Guru!

~ PodPublishing, Editors

Introduction to Shri Guru Gita

I'd like to talk about the text of the Guru Gita. When you go to India you see that there is an incredible tradition of spiritual training. We have very little of that tradition here in the West. Baba Muktananda's mission to the West, which was conceived of by his Guru Bhagawan Nityananda, began a process of what I have referred to in the past as "Shaktipat on sight". In the past, the contact and impact between Guru and disciple was very much shrouded in secrecy. You entered a very secret kind of life when you came under the grace of a Siddha Guru. I believe that out of necessity, the spiritual hierarchy realized that this entire project of human awakening needed to be carried to a more aggressive level.

It was Bhagawan Nityananda, a being of unsurpassed authority in the spiritual hierarchy, who I feel was the manager on this project and put the conditions in place for the thunderbolt of awakening to move out of the relative secrecy that enshrouded it in India. Bhagawan Nityananda gave rise to the permission blessing and empowered Muktananda to come to the West and give Shaktipat on sight. In other words, no background in spiritual training was required – all you had to do was meet him and want

By Mark Griffin

to be awakened. It's unbelievable to say those words and know them to be true.

Muktananda was an extraordinarily powerful Siddha and a profound Master. He was a true Sadguru. There was also a side to him that was incredibly pragmatic. He realized that most of the people with whom he came into contact didn't have even the slightest idea what they were getting involved in – just like you. Most of you don't have the slightest idea what you're involved in. I see that all the time. So, faced with the idea of striking anybody with the thunderbolt, even those who had no background, Muktananda hit upon the idea of the recitation of the Shri Guru Gita every morning. It is an unbelievably profound text and you simply recite it everyday.

If I were to define my sadhana, I could find no clearer description of the awakening process that I underwent, than the Guru Gita. Step by step, idea by idea, principle by principle, it is an incredibly profound document and it has the ability to make what is very difficult and mysterious, seem available and understandable.

Introduction to Shri Guru Gita

In its essence, the Guru Gita is a diagram of the method by which the awakening process occurs. It describes the transmission of Shaktipat from the Guru to the disciple, which is the entire principle behind the Whispered Lineage. The Siddha Path is known as a Whisper Lineage or a Whisper Tradition. It is not written down and this very mysterious process of awakening of a human being emerges from the impact between the Guru and the disciple. The Guru Gita is essentially a mantra by and of the nature of the Guru. The mechanics of a mantra are such that the name of the mantra, the deity of the mantra, and the power of the mantra are a single thing. Therefore, the Guru Gita is a complete description of the nature of the Guru, how the Guru operates and the mysterious method by which any person can come into contact with the Guru and receive the force of the transmission.

Again, the principle is contact. The bringing together of the Guru and the disciple produces the effect of awakening. This Shaktipat transmission is authorized by Shiva himself, and so carries his full authority. Shiva is the Lord of the Guru Shakti. In this world system, at this particular time and place, he is the ruling force. The nature of Shiva is one of centrifugal dispersion, a very wrathful spinning away and decompression of all qualities into emptiness. That's why they say that Shiva is the fast path.

By comparison, the principle of God that is known as Vishnu is one of universal cohesion, with all qualities being brought together into an infinite compression. In previous times we've heard about human beings who lived incredible long life spans when the process of awakening quite literally took centuries. This was when the ruling force was Vishnu driven. Vishnu, who is said to be the true face of God, is now fourteen of sixteen parts Shiva, so it's a Shiva dominating Vishnu principle that's active right now in our world system.

Baba was a Siddha and a Shiva Guru. That's always a code. If a Guru is described as a Siddha, it means they're outside a tradition, and spontaneously arise as enlightenment. They are the manifestation of a Whisper Lineage or a Whisper Tradition, and engage in the direct transmission from the Guru to the disciple. If a Guru is described as a Shiva Guru, that means that the path is the shortest possible way, because all qualities are dispersed instantaneously. If

Introduction to Shri Guru Gita

a Guru is described as a Siddha AND a Shiva Guru, it is code for the swiftest way one can move through the process of awakening. All of those principles are present here in Hard Light and it is how Hard Light operates.

It is extremely auspicious that the Guru Gita has emerged and is now becoming a part of the margena, the pathway of awakening here in Hard Light. The practice around Baba was very simple. Do the mantra, love God, welcome people. Simple. The practice here in Hard Light is also very simple – we do pretty much the same. Awareness of the SoHam. Constant exposure to the Kundalini. Come and see the teacher as frequently as you can. And out of that process, the awakening emerges. But I also now want to add the daily recitation of the Guru Gita.

I think it's important that the Guru Gita be recited in English, because that's our main language and more than anything, it's essential that the meaning be understood. Baba started operating inside America in 1974 and an English version of the Gita was present as a subtext, but it was principally recited in Sanskrit. In the Hard Light recitation we focus on the English

By Mark Griffin

translation, because the power emerges from clearly understanding the meaning.

There is something about the way we are as people, as human beings, that even the most important truths can be easily forgotten. We're faced with so much every day and we get rubbed very thin sometimes by the intensity of the maya. As a student of Hard Light, you're always being reminded to hold to your discipline and plunge inward. Now you can use the recitation of the Guru Gita as a supremely powerful tool that provides an opportunity for the Guru to speak directly to you. You can see and feel how powerful it is to align yourself with the Guru and the Guru Principle, the external Guru of cause and the internal Guru of action, within you and without. It gives you the ability to punch through the proliferating obscurations of kleisha-born afflictive emotion, which is always a very fierce opponent. There are also very specific applications for protection, empowerment, the clearing of obstacles, the renewal of the heart and the purification of body, mind and spirit.

In the recitation of the Guru Gita, you align with the Guru's force in the deepest way, across the entire

Introduction to Shri Guru Gita

spectrum of the expressions of Pinda, Pada, Rupa and Rupatita, as mentioned in verses 74-76. Those words embody principles beyond understanding, and it's why the Guru is the Guru. Your life is impacted with Pinda, the divine Kundalini Shaktipat; Pada, the SoHam, which is the coming together of the ocean of consciousness and the creation inside your own being; Rupa, the Blue Pearl, the true form of consciousness that is the recognition of the true Self; and Rupatita, emptiness beyond all qualities, the unfoldment of infinite consciousness as the individual and universal identities dissolve into each other and become forever one.

I wanted to introduce Shri Guru Gita on this celebration of Baba Muktananda's 26th anniversary of his Mahasamadhi. And I want it to become a part of your daily sadhana. It takes just 30 minutes to recite, and you can read the text out loud or silently to yourself. It's going to be recited everyday at the Hard Light retreat site, Fire Mountain in Nimboli, India.

The impact of the recitation of the Guru Gita acts as a powerful point of alignment with the Vajra Guru principle – that principle of mercy and awakening

By Mark Griffin

that is one and the same with God. It brings the full force of the Siddha Lineage into your life. You can be having the usual trials and tribulations and by just sitting down and reciting the Guru Gita, a wash of force will go through you that will bring you clear. This is available to you now through this daily recitation.

Mark Duffy

October 12, 2008
Lake Arrowhead, CA

Salutations to the Lord SadaShiva who is the divine source of these mantras.

The Guru, the Supreme Atman, is its deity.

Ham is its seed, *Sa* is its power and *Krom* is the anchor that holds the syllables of the mantras together.

I recite the Guru Gita now to draw the Guru's grace.

1) Knowing that Lord Shiva held the secret of Guru Yoga, the Goddess Parvati bowed to him with reverence on the summit of Mount Kailas and said:

2) O Great Lord, O Ruler of all the worlds, I long to know the path that will lead me to Awakening. Please have compassion on me. Show me the way, O Supreme Teacher of the Universe. I bow to your feet My Lord.

3) Lord Ishvara said:
O Beloved, you are my very Self. Your love and devotion draw from me this secret knowledge, inspired by your longing, which is so rare.

4. Here is the secret knowledge that is difficult to attain in the three worlds. Listen to it carefully as I reveal it to you now. The Absolute is the same as the Guru. This is the truth, O beautiful One, this is the truth.

5. The Guru is the same as the Self, the same as Consciousness itself. This is the truth. This is the absolute truth. Those who seek wisdom should make every effort to find their Guru.

6. Let me explain to you how an embodied soul becomes Enlightened. By offering seva at the feet of the Guru and drawing his grace, all obscurations are purified.

7) I shall describe to you a form of meditation that grants boons, generates happiness, and bestows Bhukti, which is worldly fulfillment, and Mukti, which is spiritual awakening. O great Goddess, listen to this teaching with one-pointed concentration.

8) Think of the Guru with every action you perform. If you sprinkle water on your head while remembering the lotus feet of Shri Guru, you obtain the same benefits as bathing in all the places of pilgrimage.

9) Always meditate on the Guru's form. Sip from the Guru's water and eat from the food that he has left. Constantly repeat the mantra he has given you.

10. The Guru is the gateway to liberation, like Varanasi, like the Ganges, and the holy banyan tree Akshaya. The Guru is himself Vishveshvara – the Shiva of Varanasi, with the Ganges at his feet. He is the Prayag, the confluence of the three holy rivers at the pilgrimage center of Gaya. Pranam to the Guru again and again.

11. Continually remember the Guru's form. Repeat his name and follow his command – think of nothing but the Guru.

12. Letting go of all attachment to your social status, your reputation and your comforts – think of nothing but the Guru.

13) If you think of nothing else but Me, you will easily reach the highest state of Realization. Thus, focus one-pointedly on merging with the Guru.

14) The word Guru is composed of two sacred syllables. Gu, which represents the darkness and Ru, which represents light. Gu is maya and Ru is the destruction of maya. Gu is the state which is beyond the three gunas, and Ru is emptiness.

The Guru is he who gives the experience of darkness melting into light, maya dissolving into clarity and formation revealing wisdom.

15) O Devi, the supreme mantra is indeed the word 'Guru', and its two letters gu and ru. The essence of the Smritis and Vedas decree that the Guru is the personification of the Highest Reality.

16) This pure king of mantras is a fire blazing in the mind – burning day and night, it removes the illusion that you are this body, thus freeing you from death itself.

17) There is no truth higher than the Guru Tattva, the Guru principle. Even gods and other celestial beings cannot attain this highest of states. A sadhaka should offer the Guru a seat, a bed, clothing and other things that will please him.

18) Pranam fully to the Guru with complete abandon and let your every action, thought and word be offered to the Guru. Serve the Guru in every way and dedicate your life to him.

19) The Guru knows you inside and out. O Beautiful One, withhold no part of yourself from him, neither that which you think of as pure nor that which you think of as dark and foul – including the germs and worms of your body, and the blood, skin and flesh, all of which are finally reduced to ashes.

20. The most powerful yoga, O Noble One, is not the pranayama with its windy breathing exercises, nor hatha yoga with its challenging and difficult positions – rather, it is the Guru Yoga, the supreme yoga, which grants the spontaneous state, whereby the powerful prana becomes still of its own accord, without effort.

21. I bow to my Guru who rescued those who were sinking in the mire of samsara, the ocean of hell, and were striving for liberation by seeking to climb the tree of life.

22. I bow to the Guru who is Brahma, who is Vishnu, who is Lord Shiva and who is indeed Parabrahman — the Ocean of Consciousness.

23. I bow to my Guru who is Shiva, the prime tattva, the only bridge across the ocean of samsara. As the master of all knowledge, he knows that by which all else is known.

24. I bow to my Guru who opened my eyes, that were blinded by the darkness of ignorance, and revealed to me the light of knowledge.

25) In order to cross over the abyss of samsara, I recognize you as my father, my mother, my brother and my God. I bow to you, my beloved Sadguru.

26) The source of meditation is the Guru's form.
The source of devotion is the Guru's feet.
The source of mantra is the Guru's word.
The source of awakening is the Guru's grace.

27) I fold my hands and bow to you my Guru, the Ocean of Benevolence, for it is only by your grace that I can be freed from the wheel of cyclic existence.

28. Through the Reality of the Guru there is truth, from the Light of the Guru there is luminosity, through the Bliss of the Guru there is joy. I bow to you, O Sadguru.

29. I bow to my Guru, who exists to reveal the truth, who ceaselessly shines like the sun to light our way, and who opens our hearts to love all those who are dear to us.

30. It is the Guru who illuminates the mind, not the mind that illuminates the Guru. I bow to my Guru who is the supreme witness of waking, dreaming and deep sleep states.

31) One whose mind is filled with thought, knows not; one whose mind is silent, knows everything. I bow to the Guru, who is one with the Absolute.

32) Goddess Parvati, only the Guru can remove the fear of aging and the dread of death. The Guru offers protection to his disciples, even if they are cursed by the sages, demons or gods.

33) If Shiva is angry, the Guru protects you. If Vishnu is angry, the Guru saves you. But if the Guru is angry, there's nowhere to hide. Therefore strive to the utmost to take refuge in the Guru's grace.

34) O Beloved, those who know say the Guru is Shiva, the witness of all, but without his three eyes; he is Vishnu, but without his four arms; he is Brahma, but without his four faces.

35) There is no difference between the contemplation of your own Guru and the contemplation of infinite Lord Shiva. Indeed, chanting the name of your own Guru is as powerful as chanting the mantra of infinite Lord Shiva.

36) The absolute form of the Guru is like nectar to those who can truly see. To those who cannot see through the veil of illusion, the true form of the Guru is shrouded, like the sunrise is to a blind man.

37) Realizing that the Guru, the Supreme Being, encompasses the entire universe, whether sentient or insentient, from a blade of grass to Lord Brahma – I honor everything, by remembering my Guru.

38) I bow to my Guru, who knows there is no second reality – only one unified field arising everywhere simultaneously. This is the truth. To see otherwise is to be fooled by the illusion of cause and effect.

39) I bow to my Guru's two lotus feet, which destroy the painful delusion of duality and always protect me from misfortune.

40. The stream of Shakti from the Guru's lotus feet removes all obstacles, lights the flame of knowledge and takes one across the ocean of samsara, the endless cycle of birth, decay, death and rebirth.

41. Bow to the Guru's feet and imbibe his essence. Thus you will attain knowledge and detachment. The karmas, which are at the root of your ignorance, will be destroyed and the cycle of rebirth will be brought to an end.

42. O Beloved, pranam with love to the Guru's feet every day, making an offering of prayers and devotion to him wherever he may be.

He is always fully awake and at one with Pure Consciousness, witnessing the drama of myriad world systems arising and dissolving.

43. I bow to the two lotus feet of my Guru, one white, embodying Shiva; one red, embodying Shakti. My speech and mind focus on the contemplation of this divine mystery.

44. Even a few particles of dust from my Guru's feet are enough to build a bridge for me to cross over the vast ocean of samsara.

Even one–thousandth part of a single drop of water that has touched the Guru's feet equals the boon of bathing in all of the holy waters across the seven seas. To the Guru I bow.

45. Luminous with the wisdom of Vedanta, like the sun continually radiating its light, the Guru's lotus feet emanate the great Truths, the crest jewels of the four Vedas:

Tat Tvam Asi
 – I Am That,

Prajñanam Brahman
 – Consciousness is Brahman,

Aham Brahmaasmi
 – I Am Brahman,

Ayam Atma Brahman
 – The Self is Brahman.

46. The Guru's lotus feet are in the mandala of the moon in Brahmarandhra, in the thousand petal chakra at the crown of the head. The cooling essence of the moon extinguishes the raging fires of worldly existence.

47. Residing in the center of the thousand petals is a divine triangle formed by the Sanskrit alphabet, with the letters A, Ka and Tha at each point. One should meditate on the Guru's two lotus feet, which are Ham and Sa, in the center of this sacred triangle.

48. In the early morning, call on the Guru and meditate on the peace within his two eyes. See him seated in the white lotus of the sahasrar, with two arms granting boons and fearlessness.

49. In the heart is a cave the size of a thumb, which is the seat of the causal body. Listen, and I shall speak to you of the meditation on this form of consciousness.

50) Seated upon a throne in the center of the heart lotus is the Guru, effulgent and luminous like the crescent of the moon.

In one hand he holds the book of knowledge, while his other hand showers boons. One should meditate upon the Guru's divine form.

51) The seat of the Guru resides in the center of the heart space, shining like a perfect crystal. Meditate on the Guru who eternally bestows bliss and is higher than the highest.

52 The Guru is beyond any description whatsoever. No imputed terms can describe him. Thus, the Vedas say "neti neti" – he is not this, he is not that.

Contemplate this great mystery, and continually worship him with both mind and speech.

53 Whether it moves or is stationary, whether it is sentient or insentient, it is all part of the great mandala of the Ocean of Consciousness.

I bow to you my Guru, who expresses the state of Samadhi that spontaneously knows this truth.

54) Thus the Guru reveals: "I am unborn, I am ageless, beginningless and deathless. I am smaller than the smallest and larger than the largest. I move and move not. I am far as well as near. I am inside everything and outside everything all at once. I am beyond cause and effect. I am the supreme Akasha. I am consciousness and bliss, never–ending, self–luminous, imperishable and pure."

55) I bow to my Guru, who is Absolute Consciousness, who is eternal, who is peace personified, who is completely pure, and who transcends the limits of space. He is beyond the primordial sound of Nada. He is beyond the Blue Pearl, Bindu. He is beyond the concentrated bliss of Kala.

56) I bow to my Guru, who is the embodiment of the jñana-shakti, the power of knowledge. The thirty-six tattvas are his garland. He bestows Bhukti – worldly happiness, and Mukti – spiritual awakening.

57) I bow to my Guru, who bestows atma-jñana, the knowledge of the Self. He burns away all the karmas carried forward from countless lifetimes.

58) I bow to my Guru, who embodies the great Guru Tattva, the universal principle of the Guru, the highest truth and the greatest austerity. There is nothing worth knowing that is more important than this.

59) My Guru is the Lord of the Universe. My Guru is the Guru of the Three Worlds. My Self is the Universal Atman. To my Guru, I bow.

60) The Guru, the first impulse of creation, is eternal and without end. He is without question the supreme of all deities. Nothing exists which is greater than he. To my Sadguru, I bow.

61) Merely recalling my Guru, knowledge arises spontaneously. Remembering him brings all attainments automatically. By meditating on the Guru in this way, the prasad of my Guru's grace delivers me to Realization.

62. I bow to my Guru who is the infinite Ocean of Consciousness, beyond perception, beyond duality, beyond the three gunas and all formation. He is the embodiment of the bliss of Brahman and the bestower of ultimate happiness.

He is ekam – one; he is nityam – eternal; he is vimalam – free from impurities; he is achalam – steadfast. He is the abode of knowledge and bliss, and is forever omniscient, omnipresent and vast like the sky. He is the witness.

To realize the great Vedantic mahavakya "Tat Tvam Asi", "Thou Art That", is to become one with the Guru.

63. Just as a crystal reflected in a mirror, replicates its shining image, in the same way, when the infinite Ocean of Consciousness is seen in the Atman, the bliss of realization dawns and the awareness of SoHam arises – "I Am That".

64. By following the Guru margena, the path of the Guru, and meditating upon him, one obtains jñana – knowledge, as well as vijñana – insight. There is nothing greater than the Guru.

65. By following the Guru's path, one's mind becomes purified. Thus one is then able to detach from the transitory objects of the world, and be free from the binding influence of false identification.

66) By following the Guru margena, one attains the highest goal – the realization of the bliss of Atman. This is generated through prasad, the gift of the Guru's grace.

67) I remember my Shri Guru, who is the supreme Brahman.

I speak of my Shri Guru, who is the supreme Brahman.

I bow to my Shri Guru, who is the supreme Brahman.

I worship my Shri Guru, who is the supreme Brahman.

68. To the eternal Shri Guru I bow. He is bliss incarnate, exuding joy. His countenance radiates ecstasy. He is awake with knowledge of his own Self.

The yogis worship him as their Lord. With the precision of a surgeon, he extricates us from the wheel of cyclic existence.

69. I bow to the Guru, who embodies Lord Bhairava, constantly revealing the five functions of creation, maintenance, dissolution, concealment and the bestowal of grace.

70. O great Goddess, one's behavior with the Guru is of utmost importance. One should never behave egotistically before the Guru. Never tell a lie to the Guru or speak discourteously to him.

Never speak ill of the Guru or forsake him, even if you don't understand his actions.

Remember the Guru for all eternity. If you ignore this teaching, in spite of hearing it, you will risk a most dreadful fate, which will last as long as the sun and moon both shine.

71) It is not the knowledge of ancient scriptures, such as the Vedas and Smritis, nor is the wearing of the clothing of a monk, that makes a true seeker. A genuine sadhu is a servant and disciple of his Guru.

72) Through the mystery of Shaktipat, the light of the Guru kindles the light within his disciple, just as one candle is used to light another candle.

The descent of grace opens the way for the disciple to realize that everything is the Ocean of Consciousness, which is beyond the perception of the senses, omnipresent, eternal, beyond imputed terms and without form.

73) A disciple becomes one with Brahman by meditating on the Guru. In this way, the stages of Samadhi undoubtedly unfold – pinda, pada and rupa.

74) Parvati asked:
O Lord Shankara, please explain these terms to me – What are pinda, pada and rupa? And is there more beyond them?

75) Lord Shiva answered:
Kundalini Shakti is pinda, the attainment of Shaktipat. Hamsa is pada, when the awareness of SoHam becomes unbroken. Bindu is rupa, the enduring vision of the Blue Pearl. And there is also rupatita, beyond rupa, known as niranjanam – merging with pure Being.

76) O my beautiful one, pinda, pada and rupa are each a specific landmark on the path of liberation, but the highest liberation is found in rupatitam, that transcendental awareness of Pure Consciousness.

77) Goddess Parvati, know Brahman, the Supreme Reality, the Great Void. It is without quality, without form, without name, without sound and beyond perception and understanding.

78) Merge into unity with Pure Consciousness and attain oneness with all. As you find everything arising simultaneously within you, you realize only this supreme principle alone exists.

79) The way the individual soul merges into universal consciousness is like the water of many rivers merging into the ocean, or like the space inside and outside a clay pot finally being perceived as the same space.

80) This is the state of realization, when the individual embodied soul merges into the supreme Self. Having established unity consciousness, he celebrates this oneness day and night, always blissful, always tranquil, wherever he may be.

81) After attaining this solitary and tranquil state, through the grace of the Guru, all your attachments and desires dissolve into nothing.

82) He who attains the realization of Brahman, the highest knowledge, indeed becomes the Guru. Then, without a doubt, wherever he goes, he experiences the divine.

83) Then the life of a fully liberated person of wisdom becomes filled with devotion. He focuses his every effort on service to God.

84) He is free from worries, and Bhukti and Mukti are his to enjoy – worldly fulfillment and liberation.

O Parvati, his tongue is graced with Saraswati, the Goddess of speech, learning and knowledge.

85) The supreme purity and taintless quality of the Guru draw all that is holy to him – so the place where he lives naturally becomes sanctified and filled with a multitude of deities.

In these ways, O Goddess, I have described the nature of a liberated person to you.

86) O Devi, by following the path of the Guru, I have clearly shown you how to achieve this liberation through devotion to the Guru and through meditation on the Guru.

87) O Wise One, much can be accomplished through these spiritual practices. Focus your attention on service and working for the welfare of people, instead of using your accrued Shakti for self–centered worldly gain.

88) Without knowledge of Brahman, all your actions are worldly and continue to spool on more and more karma, sinking you further into the ocean of samsara. A knower of truth has unspooled all his karma, and all his subsequent actions are no longer binding and collect no further karma.

89. O Devi, this truth which I have revealed to you takes the form of the Guru Gita. Repeat it often to remove the binding influence of the wheel of cyclic existence.

90. Contemplate this Guru Gita with devotion – read it, listen to the Guru recite it, journal about it. This will yield the fruit of liberation.

91. Recite the Guru Gita. Each and every letter is an empowered mantra. Other mantras do not have the merit of even one-sixteenth part of it.

92) Bountiful rewards are obtained by repeating the Guru Gita. The recitation removes all obstacles and ends all suffering and hardship.

93) It removes the fear of time and death, and is the destroyer of all adversity, while protecting one from the influence of wild spirits, demons, ghosts and thieves.

94) It removes the disease of worldly existence. It bestows riches and siddhis, as well as the ability to influence others. Always repeat the Guru Gita.

95) Through this repetition, one becomes free from bondage, gains the favor of all the Gods and attains Lordship of the deities of Consciousness.

96) The Guru Gita brings one into direct contact with the pillar of the Siddha lineage. It brings the refined, spiritual qualities of sattva guna to the forefront. It increases good karma and dissolves bad karma.

97) Repeating the Guru Gita aligns one's life with the Guru. It brings good dreams to fruition and curtails bad dreams. Fear of the astrological influence of the nine planets is diminished; and unfinished tasks become easy to complete.

98) It removes all obstacles and quickens the fulfillment of desires. It accomplishes the four-fold goals of life:
   Dharma – righteous duty;
   Artha – wealth;
   Kama – pleasure;
   Moksha – liberation.

99) If one's goal is liberation, the Guru Gita should be recited regularly. The glory of liberation will be attained, as well as the fruition of worldly desire.

100) Repeat the Guru Gita and bathe in the cleansing waters of the ocean of truth, thus washing away the impurities of the world and the binding trap of samsara, the cycle of birth and death.

101. Having established inner silence of the mind, repeat the Guru Gita with detachment, in a clean and sacred place.

Now I shall speak of the places that are beneficial for this spiritual practice:

At the seashore, along a river, in all holy temples and shrines such as those to Shiva, Shakti or Vishnu, in a cowshed, by sacred trees, such as the dhatri or mango, thorn–apple or banyan, in a grove of tulsi plants, or in an ashram. O Beautiful One, it is also fruitful to repeat the Guru Gita in a cemetery or in frightening desolate places.

102) O Devi, prepare your seat well, with the proper asana. Use a white woolen blanket placed over kusha or durva grass, to reap the highest attainments. Or use a tiger skin or black deer skin, which give rise to liberation and knowledge. Other seats are not as favorable for your practice, such as cloth, wood or sitting directly on the ground.

103) How you position your seat is also important. To influence others, sit on a red seat facing east. To defeat demons, sit on a black seat facing south. To gain wealth, sit on a yellow seat facing west. But the highest outcome is achieved when you recite the Guru Gita facing north on a white seat, and realize peace.

104. Satyam. Satyam. The Guru Gita is the truth. There is nothing else like it, O Beautiful One.

I have revealed this truth to you in answer to your longing.

This is the truth.
This is the truth.

105. O Goddess, the dedication of one's life to the Guru is extraordinary. Everything is affected by this devotion – the devotee's mother, father, family and ancestry are all blessed. Even the earth itself rejoices.

106 Complete immersion in the Guru – Gurubhava – is the most holy pilgrimage. Going to any other place of pilgrimage is hollow and futile. O Parvati, why go somewhere else to worship, when the big toe of the Guru's foot is the ultimate abode of all that is sacred.

107 Beyond the Guru there is nothing.
Beyond the Guru there is nothing.
Beyond the Guru there is nothing.
Beyond the Guru there is nothing.

This is the word of Shiva.
This is the word of Shiva.
This is the word of Shiva.
This is the word of Shiva.

108) Indeed, the Guru Gita is Shiva.
The Guru Gita is Shiva.
The Guru Gita is Shiva.
The Guru Gita is indeed Shiva.

This is my supreme command.
This is my supreme command.
This is my supreme command.
This is my supreme command.

And so ends the Guru Gita – the discourse given by Lord Shiva to his consort, the Goddess Parvati, and recorded in the text of the Shri Skanda Purana.

I offer this Guru Gita at the revered lotus feet of my Guru.

ॐ अस्य श्रीगुरुगीतास्तोत्रमन्त्रस्य
भगवान् सदाशिव ऋषिः नानाविधानि
छन्दांसि । श्रीगुरुपरमात्मा देवता ॥

Om asya shri gurugitaa stotra mantrasya bhagavaan sadaashiva rshih. Naana vidhaani chandaamsi shri guru paramaatmaa devataa.

Om. Salutations to the Lord Sadashiva who is the divine source of these mantras. The guru, the Supreme Atman, is its deity.

हं बीजम् । सः शक्तिः । क्रों कीलकम् ।
श्रीगुरुप्रसादसिद्ध्यर्थे जपे विनियोगः ॥

Ham bijam sah shaktih krom kilakam shri guru prasaada siddhyarthe jape viniyogaha.

ham is its seed, sa is its power and krom is the anchor that holds the syllables of the mantras together. I recite the guru gita now to draw the guru's grace.

1) कैलासशिखरे रम्ये भक्तिसन्धाननायकम् ।
प्रणम्य पार्वती भक्त्या शङ्करं पर्यपृच्छत ॥

Kailaasa shikhare ramye, bhakti sandhaana naayakam; Pranamya paarvati bhaktyaa, shankaram parya prchata.

knowing that lord shiva held the secret of guru yoga, the goddess parvati bowed to him with reverence on the summit of mount kailas and said:

2)

श्रीदेव्युवाच
ॐ नमो देवदेवेश परात्पर जगद्गुरो।
सदाशिव महादेव गुरुदीक्षां प्रदेहि मे।
केन मार्गेण भो स्वामिन् देहि ब्रह्ममयो भवेत्।
त्वं कृपां कुरु मे स्वामिन् नमामि चरणौ तव॥

Shri devyuvaccha:

Om namo deva devesha, paraatpara jagad guro;
Sadaashiva mahaadeva, guru dikshaam pradehi me.

Kena maargena bho svaamin, dehi brahmamayo
bhavet; Twam krpaam kuru may svaamin,
namaami charanau tava.

O great lord, O ruler of all the worlds, I long to know the path that will lead me to awakening.

Please have compassion on me. Show me the way, O supreme teacher of the universe. I bow to your feet my lord.

3)
ईश्वर उवाच
मम रूपासि देवि त्वं त्वत्प्रीत्यर्थं वदाम्यहम् ।
लोकोपकारकः प्रश्नो न केनापि कृतः पुरा ॥

Ishvara uvacha:
Mama rupaasi devi tvam, tvat prityartham vadaam yaham; Loko pakaarakah prashno, na kenaapi krtah puraa.

Lord Ishvara said:
O beloved, you are my very Self. Your love and devotion draw from me this secret knowledge, inspired by your longing, which is so rare.

4)
दुर्लभं त्रिषु लोकेषु तच्छृणुष्व वदाम्यहम् ।
गुरुं विना ब्रह्म नान्यत् सत्यं सत्यं वरानने ॥

Durlabham trishu lokeshu, tach chrnushva vadaamyaham; Gurum vinaa Brahma naanyat, satyam satyam varaanane.

Here is the secret knowledge that is difficult to attain in the three worlds. Listen to it carefully as I reveal it to you now. The Absolute is the same as the guru. This is the truth, O beautiful one, this is the truth.

5) गुरुबुद्ध्यात्मनो नान्यत् सत्यं सत्यं न संशयः।
तल्लाभार्थं प्रयत्नस्तु कर्तव्यो हि मनीषिभिः॥

Guru buddhyaat mano naanyat, satyam satyam
na samshayaha; Tallaa bhaartham prayat nastu,
kartavyo hi manishibhihi.

The guru is the same as the Self, the same as
Consciousness itself. This is the truth. This is the
absolute truth. Those who seek wisdom should
make every effort to find their guru.

6) सर्वपापविशुद्धात्मा श्रीगुरोः पादसेवनात्।
देही ब्रह्म भवेद्यस्मात् त्वत्कृपार्थं वदामि ते॥

Sarva paapa vishuddhaatmaa, shri guroh paada
sevanaat; Dehi brahma bhaved yasmaat, tvat
krpaartham vadaami te.

Let me explain to you how an embodied soul
becomes Enlightened. By offering seva at the
feet of the guru and drawing his grace, all
obscurations are purified.

7) ध्यानं शृणु महादेवि सर्वानन्दप्रदायकम् ।
सर्वसौख्यकरं नित्यं भुक्तिमुक्तिविधायकम् ॥

Dhyaanam shrnu mahaadevi, sarvaananda pradaayakam; Sarva saukhya karam nityam, bhukti mukti vidhaayakam.

I shall describe to you a form of meditation that grants boons, generates happiness, and bestows bhukti, which is worldly fulfillment, and mukti, which is spiritual awakening. O great goddess, listen to this teaching with one-pointed concentration.

8) गुरुपादाम्बुजं स्मृत्वा जलं शिरसि धारयेत् ।
सर्वतीर्थावगाहस्य सम्प्राप्नोति फलं नरः ॥

Guru paadaam bujam smrtvaa, jalam shirasi dhaarayet; Sarva tirthaa vagaahasya, sampraapnoti phalam naraha.

Think of the guru with every action you perform. If you sprinkle water on your head while remembering the lotus feet of Shri Guru, you obtain the same benefits as bathing in all the places of pilgrimage.

9) गुरोः पादोदकं पीत्वा गुरोरुच्छिष्टभोजनम् ।
गुरुमूर्तेः सदा ध्यानं गुरुमन्त्रं सदा जपेत् ॥

Guroh paado dakam pitvaa, guro rucchishta bhojanam; Guru murte sadaa dhyaanam, guru mantram sadaa japet.

Always meditate on the guru's form. Sip from the guru's water and eat from the food that he has left. Constantly repeat the mantra he has given you.

10) काशीक्षेत्रं तन्निवासो जाह्नवी चरणोदकम् ।
गुरुर्विश्वेश्वरः साक्षात् तारकं ब्रह्म निश्चितम् ।
गुरोः पादोदकं यत्तु गयाऽसौ सोऽक्षयो वटः ।
तीर्थराजः प्रयागश्च गुरुमूर्त्यै नमो नमः ॥

Kaashi kshetram tannivaaso, jaahnavi charano dakam; Gurur vishveshvarah saakshaat, taarakam brahma nishchitam. Guroh paado dakam yattu, gayaa sau saukshayo vataha; Tirtha raaja prayaagash cha, gurumurte namo namaha.

The guru is the gateway to liberation, like Varanasi, like the Ganges, and the holy banyan tree Akshaya. The guru is himself Vishveshvara – the Shiva of Varanasi, with the Ganges at his feet. he is the Prayag, the confluence of the three holy rivers at the pilgrimage center of Gaya. Pranam to the guru again and again.

11) गुरुमूर्तिं स्मरेन्नित्यं गुरुनाम सदा जपेत् ।
गुरोराज्ञां प्रकुर्वीत गुरोरन्यन्न भावयेत् ॥

Guru murtim smarenityam, guru naama sadaa japet;
Guroraajñaam prakurvita, guror anyanna bhaavayet.

Continually remember the guru's form. Repeat his name and follow his command - think of nothing but the guru.

12) स्वाश्रमं च स्वजातिं च स्वकीर्तिपुष्टिवर्धनम् ।
एतत्सर्वं परित्यज्य गुरोरन्यन्न भावयेत् ॥

Svaa shramam cha svajaatim cha, sva kirti pushti vardhanam; Etat sarvam parityajya, guror anyanna bhaavayet.

Letting go of all attachment to your social status, your reputation and your comforts - think of nothing but the guru.

13) अनन्याश्चिन्तयन्तो मां सुलभं परमं पदम् ।
तस्मात्सर्वप्रयत्नेन गुरोराराधनं कुरु ॥

Ananyaash chintayanto maam, sulabham paramam padam; Tasmaat sarva prayatnena, guror aaraadhanam kuru.

if you think of nothing else but me, you will easily reach the highest state of realization. Thus, focus one-pointedly on merging with the guru.

14)

गुकारस्त्वन्धकारश्च रुकारस्तेज उच्यते।
अज्ञान-ग्रासकं ब्रह्म गुरुरेव न संशयः।
गुकारः प्रथमो वर्णो मायादि-गुणभासकः।
रुकारो द्वितीयो ब्रह्म मायाभ्रान्तिविनाशनम्।
गुकारं च गुणातीतं रुकारं रूपवर्जितम्।
गुणातीत-स्वरूपं च यो दद्यात्स गुरुः स्मृतः॥

Gukaaras tvandha karash cha, rukaaras teja uchyate; Ajñaana graasakam brahma, gurur eva na samshayaha. Gukaarah prathamo varno, mayaadi guna bhaasakah; Rukaaro dvitiyo brahma, maayaa bhraanti vinaashanam. Gukaaram cha gunaa titam, rukaaram rupa varjitam; Gunaatita svarupam cha, yo dadyaat sa guruh smrtah.

The word guru is composed of two sacred syllables. Gu, which represents the darkness and ru, which represents light. Gu is maya and ru is the destruction of maya. Gu is the state which is beyond the three gunas, and ru is emptiness. The guru is he who gives the experience of darkness melting into light, maya dissolving into clarity and formation revealing wisdom.

15) मन्त्रराजमिदं देवि गुरुरित्यक्षर-द्वयम् ।
स्मृतिवेदार्थवाक्येन गुरुः साक्षात्परं पदम् ॥

Mantra raajam idam devi, gurur ityakshara dvayam; Smrti vedaartha vaakyena, guruh saakshaat param padam.

O devi, the supreme mantra is indeed the word 'guru', and its two letters gu and ru. The essence of the Smritis and Vedas decree that the guru is the personification of the highest Reality.

16) अग्निशुद्धसमं तात ज्वालापरिचकाधिया ।
मन्त्रराजमिमं मन्येऽहर्निशं पातु मृत्युतः ॥

Agni shuddha samam taata, jvaalaa parichakaa dhiya; Mantra raajam imam manye, harnisham paatu mrtyutah.

This pure king of mantras is a fire blazing in the mind – burning day and night, it removes the illusion that you are this body, thus freeing you from death itself.

17)

एवं गुरुपदं श्रेष्ठं देवानामपि दुर्लभम् ।
हाहाहूहूगणैश्चैव गन्धर्वैश्च प्रपूज्यते ।
ध्रुवं तेषां च सर्वेषां नास्ति तत्त्वं गुरोः परम् ।
आसनं शयनं वस्त्रं भूषणं वाहनादिकम् ।
साधकेन प्रदातव्यं गुरु-संतोष-कारकम् ।
गुरोराधनं कार्यं स्व-जीवित्वं निवेदयेत् ॥

Evam guru padam shreshtham, devaanaamapi durlabham; Haahaa huhu ganaish chaiva, gandharvaish cha prapujyate.

Dhruvam teshaam cha sarveshaam, naasti tat tvam guroh param; Aasanam shayanam vastram, bhushanam vaahanaa dikam.

Saadhakena pradaatavyam, guru santosha kaarakam; Guror aaraadhanam kaaryam, sva jivitvam nivedayet.

There is no truth higher than the guru tattva, the guru principle. Even gods and other celestial beings cannot attain this highest of states. A sadhaka should offer the guru a seat, a bed, clothing and other things that will please him.

18) कर्मणा मनसा वाचा नित्यमाराधयेद् गुरुम् ।
दीर्घदण्डं नमस्कृत्य निर्लज्जो गुरुसन्निधौ ॥

Karmanaa manasaa vaachaa, nityam aaraadhayed gurum; Dirgha dandam namaskrtya, nirlajjo guru sannidhau.

Pranam fully to the guru with complete abandon and let your every action, thought and word be offered to the guru. Serve the guru in every way and dedicate your life to him.

19) कृमिकीटभस्मविष्ठा-दुर्गन्धिमलमूत्रकम् ।
श्लेष्मरक्तं त्वचा मांसं वञ्चयेन्न वरानने ॥

Krmi kita bhasma vishthaa, durgandhi mala mutrakam; Shleshma raktam tva chaa maamsam, vañchayenna varaanane.

The guru knows you inside and out. O beautiful one, withhold no part of yourself from him, neither that which you think of as pure nor that which you think of as dark and foul – including the germs and worms of your body, and the blood, skin and flesh, all of which are finally reduced to ashes.

20. अभ्यस्तैः सकलैः सुदीर्घमनिलैर्व्याधिप्रदैर्दुष्करैः
प्राणायाम - शतैरनेक - करणैर् दुःखात्मकैर्दुर्जयैः।
यस्मिन्नभ्युदिते विनश्यति बली वायुः स्वयं तत्क्षणात्
प्राप्तुं तत्सहजं स्वभावमनिशं सेवध्वमेकं गुरुम् ॥

Abhyastaih sakalaih sudir ghamanilair, vyaadhi pradair dushkaraih, pranaayaama shatair aneka karanair, duhkhaatmakair durjayaihi;

Yasminn abhyudite vinashyati bali, vaayuh svayam tat kshanaat, praptum tat sahajam svabhaavam anisham, sevadhvam ekam gurum.

The most powerful yoga, O noble one, is not the pranayama with its windy breathing exercises, nor hatha yoga with its challenging and difficult positions – rather, it is the guru yoga, the supreme yoga, which grants the spontaneous state, whereby the powerful prana becomes still of its own accord, without effort.

21) संसारवृक्षमारूढाः पतन्तो नरकार्णवे ।
येन चैवोद्धृताः सर्वे तस्मै श्रीगुरवे नमः ॥

Samsaara vrksham aarudhaah, patanto narakaarnave; Yena chaivo ddhrtaah sarve, tasmai shri gurave namaha.

i bow to my guru who rescued those who were sinking in the mire of samsara, the ocean of hell, and were striving for liberation by seeking to climb the tree of life.

22) गुरुर्ब्रह्मा गुरुर्विष्णुर् गुरुर्देवो महेश्वरः ।
गुरुरेव पर-ब्रह्म तस्मै श्रीगुरवे नमः ॥

Gurur brahmaa gurur vishnu, gurur devo maheshvarah; Gurur eva para brahma, tasmai shri gurave namaha.

i bow to the guru who is brahma, who is vishnu, who is lord shiva and who is indeed parabrahman - the ocean of consciousness.

23) हेतवे जगतामेव संसारार्णव-सेतवे।
प्रभवे सर्वविद्यानां शम्भवे गुरवे नमः॥

Hetave jagataam eva, samsaarar nava setave;
Prabhave sarva vidyaanaam, shambhave gurave namaha.

I bow to my guru who is Shiva, the prime tattva, the only bridge across the ocean of samsara. As the master of all knowledge, he knows that by which all else is known.

24) अज्ञानतिमिरान्धस्य ज्ञानाञ्जनशलाकया।
चक्षुरुन्मीलितं येन तस्मै श्रीगुरवे नमः॥

Ajñaana timir aandhasya, jñaanaañ jana shalaakayaa; Chakshur unmilitam yena, tasmai shri gurave namaha.

I bow to my guru who opened my eyes, that were blinded by the darkness of ignorance, and revealed to me the light of knowledge.

25) त्वं पिता त्वं च मे माता त्वं बन्धुस्त्वं च देवता।
संसार-प्रतिबोधार्थं तस्मै श्रीगुरवे नमः॥

Tvam pitaa tvam cha me maataa, tvam bandhus tvam cha devataa; Samsaara prati bodhaartham, tasmai shri gurave namaha.

In order to cross over the abyss of samsara, I recognize you as my father, my mother, my brother and my god. I bow to you, my beloved Sadguru.

26) ध्यानमूलं गुरोर्मूर्तिः पूजामूलं गुरोः पदम्।
मन्त्रमूलं गुरोर्वाक्यं मोक्षमूलं गुरोः कृपा॥

Dhyaana mulam guror murtih, pujaa mulam guroh padam; Mantra mulam guror vaakyam, moksha mulam guroh krpaa.

The source of meditation is the Guru's form.
The source of devotion is the Guru's feet.
The source of mantra is the Guru's word.
The source of awakening is the Guru's grace.

27) अयं मयाञ्जलिर्बद्धो दयासागरवृद्धये।
यदनुग्रहतो जन्तुश्चित्रसंसारमुक्तिभाक् ॥

Ayam mayaañ jalir baddho, dayaa saagara vrddhaye; Yad anugrahato jantush, chitra samsaara muktibhaak.

I fold my hands and bow to you my guru, the ocean of benevolence, for it is only by your grace that I can be freed from the wheel of cyclic existence.

28) यत्सत्येन जगत्सत्यं यत्प्रकाशेन भाति तत्।
यदानन्देन नन्दन्ति तस्मै श्रीगुरवे नमः॥

Yat satyena jagat satyam, yat prakaashena bhaati tat; Yad aanandena nandanti, tasmai shri gurave namaha.

Through the reality of the guru there is truth, from the light of the guru there is luminosity, through the bliss of the guru there is joy. I bow to you, O sadguru.

29) यस्य स्थित्या सत्यमिदं यद्भाति भानुरूपतः ।
प्रियं पुत्रादि यत्प्रीत्या तस्मै श्रीगुरवे नमः ॥

Yasya sthithyaa satyam idam, yad bhaati bhaanu rupatah; Priyam putraadi yat prityaa, tasmai shri gurave namaha.

I bow to my guru, who exists to reveal the truth, who ceaselessly shines like the sun to light our way, and who opens our hearts to love all those who are dear to us.

30) येन चेतयते हीदं चित्तं चेतयते न यम् ।
जाग्रत्स्वप्नसुषुप्त्यादि तस्मै श्रीगुरवे नमः ॥

Yena chetayate hidam, chittam chetayate na yam; Jaagrat svapna sushuptyaadi, tasmai shri gurave namaha.

It is the guru who illuminates the mind, not the mind that illuminates the guru. I bow to my guru who is the supreme witness of waking, dreaming and deep sleep states.

31) यस्यामतं तस्य मतं मतं यस्य न वेद सः। अनन्यभावभावाय तस्मै श्रीगुरवे नमः॥

Yasyaa matam tasya matam, matam yasya na veda saha; Ananya bhaava bhaavaaya, tasmai shri gurave namaha.

One whose mind is filled with thought, knows not; one whose mind is silent, knows everything. I bow to the guru, who is one with the absolute.

32) मुनिभिः पन्नगैर्वाऽपि सुरैर्वा शापितो यदि। कालमृत्युभयाद् वापि गुरु रक्षति पार्वति॥

Munibhih pannagair vaapi, surairvaa shaapito yadi; Kaala mrtyu bhayaad vaapi, guru rakshati paarvati.

Goddess Parvati, only the guru can remove the fear of aging and the dread of death. The guru offers protection to his disciples, even if they are cursed by the sages, demons or gods.

33) शिवे क्रुद्धे गुरुस्त्राता गुरौ क्रुद्धे शिवो न हि।
तस्मात् सर्वप्रयत्नेन श्रीगुरुं शरणं व्रजेत्।
हरौ रुष्टे गुरुस्त्राता गुरौ रुष्टे न कश्चन।
तस्मात् सर्वप्रयत्नेन श्रीगुरुं शरणं व्रजेत् ॥

Shive kruddhe guru straataa, gurau kruddhe shivo na hi; Tasmaat sarva prayatnena, shri gurum sharanam vrajet.

Harau rushte guru straataa, gurau rushte na kashchana; Tasmaat sarva prayatnena, shri gurum sharanam vrajet.

If Shiva is angry, the guru protects you. If Vishnu is angry, the guru saves you. But if the guru is angry, there's nowhere to hide. Therefore strive to the utmost to take refuge in the guru's grace.

34) अत्रिनेत्रः सर्वसाक्षी अचतुर्बाहुरच्युतः।
अचतुर्वदनो ब्रह्मा श्रीगुरुः कथितः प्रिये ॥

Atrinetrah sarva saakshi, achatur baahur achyutah; Achatur vadano brahmaa, shri guruh kathitah priye.

O beloved, those who know say the guru is Shiva, the witness of all, but without his three eyes; he is Vishnu, but without his four arms; he is brahma, but without his four faces.

35)
स्वदेशिकस्यैव शरीरचिन्तनं
भवेदनन्तस्य शिवस्य चिन्तनम् ।
स्वदेशिकस्यैव च नामकीर्तनं
भवेदनन्तस्य शिवस्य कीर्तनम् ॥

Sva deshika syaiva sharira chintanam,
bhaved anantasya shivasya chintanam;
Sva deshika syaiva cha naama kirtanam,
bhaved anantasya shivasya kirtanam.

There is no difference between the contemplation of your own guru and the contemplation of infinite lord Shiva. Indeed, chanting the name of your own guru is as powerful as chanting the mantra of infinite lord Shiva.

36)

श्रीगुरोः परमं रूपं विवेक-चक्षुषोऽमृतम् ।
मन्दभाग्या न पश्यन्ति अन्धाः सूर्योदयं यथा ॥

Shri guroh paramam rupam, viveka chakshusho mrtam; Manda bhaagyaa na pashyanti, andhah suryo dayam yathaa.

The absolute form of the guru is like nectar to those who can truly see. To those who cannot see through the veil of illusion, the true form of the guru is shrouded, like the sunrise is to a blind man.

37)

आब्रह्मस्तम्बपर्यन्तं परमात्मस्वरूपकम् ।
स्थावरं जङ्गमं चैव प्रणमामि जगन्मयम् ॥

Aabrahma stamba paryantam, paramaatma svarupakam; Sthaavaram jangamam chaiva, pranamaami jagan mayam.

Realizing that the guru, the supreme being, encompasses the entire universe, whether sentient or insentient, from a blade of grass to lord brahma - I honor everything, by remembering my guru.

38)

नानारूपमिदं सर्वं न केनाप्यस्ति भिन्नता ।
कार्यकारणता चैव तस्मै श्रीगुरवे नमः ॥

Naanaa rupam idam sarvam, na kenaa pyasti bhinnataa; Kaarya kaaranataa chaiva, tasmai shri gurave namaha.

I bow to my guru, who knows there is no second reality – only one unified field arising everywhere simultaneously. This is the truth. To see otherwise is to be fooled by the illusion of cause and effect.

39)

यदङ्घ्रि-कमलद्वन्द्वं द्वन्द्वताप-निवारकम् ।
तारकं सर्वदाऽपद्भ्यः श्रीगुरुं प्रणमाम्यहम् ॥

Yad anghri kamala dvandvam, dvandva taapa nivaarakam; Taarakam sarvadaa padbhyhah, shri gurum pranamaamyaham.

I bow to my guru's two lotus feet, which destroy the painful delusion of duality and always protect me from misfortune.

40) शोषणं पापपङ्कस्य दीपनं ज्ञानतेजसाम् ।
गुरुपादोदकं सम्यक् संसारार्णवतारकम् ॥

Shoshanam paapa pankasya, deepanam jñaana tejasaam; Guru paado dakam samyak, samsaarar nava taarakam.

The stream of Shakti from the guru's lotus feet removes all obstacles, lights the flame of knowledge and takes one across the ocean of samsara, the endless cycle of birth, decay, death and rebirth.

41) अज्ञानमूल - हरणं जन्म - कर्म - निवारणम् ।
ज्ञानवैराग्यसिद्ध्यर्थं गुरुपादोदकं पिबेत् ॥

Ajñaana mula haranam, janma karma nivaaranam; Jñaana vairaagya siddyartham, guru paado dakam pibet.

Bow to the guru's feet and imbibe his essence. Thus you will attain knowledge and detachment. The karmas, which are at the root of your ignorance, will be destroyed and the cycle of rebirth will be brought to an end.

42

श्रीनाथ - चरणद्वन्द्वं यस्यां दिशि विराजते।
तस्यै दिशे नमस्कुर्याद् भक्त्या प्रतिदिनं प्रिये।
तस्यै दिशे सततमञ्जलिरेष आर्येप्रक्षिप्यते।
मुखरितो मधुपैर्बुधैश्च जागर्ति यत्र भगवान्।
गुरुचक्रवर्ती विश्वोदयप्रलयनाटकनित्यसाक्षी॥

Shrinaatha charana dvandvam, yasyaam dishi viraajate; Tasyai dishe namas kuryaad, bhaktyaa prati dinam priye.

Tasyai dishe satatam añjaliresha aarye, prakshipyate mukharito madhupair budhaish cha; Jaagarti yatra bhagavaan guru chakra varti, vishvodaya pralaya naataka nitya saakshi.

O beloved, pranam with love to the Guru's feet every day, making an offering of prayers and devotion to him wherever he may be.

He is always fully awake and at one with pure Consciousness, witnessing the drama of myriad world systems arising and dissolving.

43) वन्दे गुरु-पदद्वन्द्वं वाङ्मनश्चित्त-गोचरम् ।
श्वेतरक्तप्रभाभिन्नं शिवशक्त्यात्मकं परम् ॥

Vande guru pada dvandvam, vaan manash citta gocharam; Shveta rakta prabhaa bhinnam, shiva shaktyaat makam param.

I bow to the two lotus feet of my guru, one white, embodying Shiva; one red, embodying Shakti. My speech and mind focus on the contemplation of this divine mystery.

44) यत्पादरेणुकणिका कापि संसारवारिधेः ।
सेतुबन्धायते नाथं देशिकं तमुपास्महे ।
सप्तसागरपर्यन्त - तीर्थस्नानादिकं फलम् ।
गुरोरङ्घ्रिपयोबिन्दु - सहस्रांशे न दुर्लभम् ॥

Yat paada renu kanikaa, kaapi samsaara vaaridheh; Setu bandhaayate naatham, deshikam tam upaasmahe. Sapta saagara paryanta, tirtha snaanaadikam phalam; Guror anghri payo bindu, sahasraamshe na durlabham.

Even a few particles of dust from my guru's feet are enough to build a bridge for me to cross over the vast ocean of samsara.

Even one-thousandth part of a single drop of water that has touched the guru's feet equals the boon of bathing in all of the holy waters across the seven seas. To the guru I bow.

45)

सर्वश्रुतिशिरोरत्न - विराजितपदाम्बुजः ।
वेदान्ताम्बुजसूर्यो यस्तस्मै श्रीगुरवे नमः ॥

Sarva shruti shiroratna, viraajita padaambujah;
Vedaantaam buja suryo yas, tasmai shri gurave namaha.

Luminous with the wisdom of Vedanta, like the sun continually radiating its light, the guru's lotus feet emanate the great truths, the crest jewels of the four Vedas:
    Tat Tvam Asi – I am that,
    Prajñanam brahman – Consciousness is
       brahman,
    Aham brahmaasmi – I am brahman,
    Ayam atma brahman – The Self is brahman.

46) पादाब्जं सर्वसंसार-दावानलविनाशकम् ।
ब्रह्मरन्ध्रे सिताम्भोज-मध्यस्थं चन्द्रमण्डले ॥

Paadaabjam sarva samsaara, daavaanala vinaashakam; Brahma randhre sitaambhoja, madhyastham chandra mandale.

The guru's lotus feet are in the mandala of the moon in brahmaranadhra, in the thousand petal chakra at the crown of the head. The cooling essence of the moon extinguishes the raging fires of worldly existence.

47) अकथादि त्रिरेखाब्जे सहस्रदलमण्डले ।
हंसपार्श्वत्रिकोणे च स्मरेत्तन्मध्यगं गुरुम् ॥

Akathaadi trirekhaabje, sahasra dala mandale; Hamsa paarshva trikone cha, smaret tan madhyagam gurum.

Residing in the center of the thousand petals is a divine triangle formed by the Sanskrit alphabet, with the letters ā, ka and tha at each point. One should meditate on the guru's two lotus feet, which are ham and sa, in the center of this sacred triangle.

48)

प्रातः शिरसि शुक्लाब्जे द्विनेत्रं द्विभुजं गुरुम् ।
वराभययुतं शान्तं स्मरेत् तं नामपूर्वकम् ॥

Praatah shirasi shuklaabje, dvinetram dvibhujam gurum; Varaa bhaya yutam shaantam, smaret tam naama purvakam.

In the early morning, call on the guru and meditate on the peace within his two eyes. See him seated in the white lotus of the sahasrar, with two arms granting boons and fearlessness.

49)

अङ्गुष्ठमात्रपुरुषं ध्यायतश्चिन्मयं हृदि ।
तत्र स्फुरति भावो यः शृणु तं कथयाम्यहम् ॥

Angushtha maatra purusham, dhyaa yatash chinmayam hrdi; Tatra sphurati bhaavo yah, shrunu tam kathayaamyaham.

In the heart is a cave the size of a thumb, which is the seat of the causal body. Listen, and I shall speak to you of the meditation on this form of consciousness.

50) हृदम्बुजे कर्णिकमध्यसंस्थे सिंहासने
संस्थितदिव्यमूर्तिम् ध्यायेद्गुरुं चन्द्रकला
प्रकाशं चित्पुस्तकाभीष्टवरं दधानम् ॥

Hrdambuje karnika madhya samsthe, simhaasane samsthita divya murtim; Dhyaayed gurum chandra kalaa prakaasham, chit pusta kaabhishta varam dadhaanam.

Seated upon a throne in the center of the heart lotus is the guru, effulgent and luminous like the crescent of the moon. In one hand he holds the book of knowledge, while his other hand showers boons. One should meditate upon the guru's divine form.

51) परात्परतरं ध्येयं नित्यमानन्दकारकम् ।
हृदयाकाशमध्यस्थं शुद्धस्फटिकसन्निभम् ॥

Paraat para taram dhyeyam, nityam aananda kaarakam; Hrdayaa kaasha madhyastham, shuddha sphatika sannibham.

The seat of the guru resides in the center of the heart space, shining like a perfect crystal. Meditate on the guru who eternally bestows bliss and is higher than the highest.

52

यस्मात्परतरं नास्ति नेति नेतीति वै श्रुतिः।
मनसा वचसा चैव नित्यमाराधयेद् गुरुम् ॥

Yasmaat para taram naasti, neti netiti vai shrutihi;
Manasaa vachasaa chaiva, nityam aaraadhayed gurum.

The guru is beyond any description whatsoever. No imputed terms can describe him. Thus, the Vedas say "neti neti" – he is not this, he is not that. Contemplate this great mystery, and continually worship him with both mind and speech.

53) अखण्डमण्डलाकारं व्याप्तं येन चराचरम् ।
तत्पदं दर्शितं येन तस्मै श्रीगुरवे नमः ।
स्थावरं जङ्गमं चैव तथा चैव चराचरम् ।
व्याप्तं येन जगत्सर्वं तस्मै श्रीगुरवे नमः ॥

Akhanda mandalaa kaaram, vyaaptam yena charaacharam; Tat padam darshitam yena, tasmai shri gurave namaha.

Sthaavaram jangamam chaiva, tatha chaiva charaacharam; Vyaaptam yena jagat sarvam, tasmai shri gurave namaha.

Whether it moves or is stationary, whether it is sentient or insentient, it is all part of the great mandala of the ocean of consciousness.
I bow to you my guru, who expresses the state of samadhi that spontaneously knows this truth.

54) तदेजति तन्नैजति तद्दूरे तत्समीपके ।
तदन्तरस्य सर्वस्य तदु सर्वस्य बाह्यतः ।
अजोऽहमजरोऽहं च अनादिनिधनः स्वयम् ।
अविकारश्चिदानन्द अणियान्महतो महान् ।
अपूर्वाणां परं नित्यं स्वयंज्योतिर्निरामयम् ।
विरजं परमाकाशं ध्रुवमानन्दमव्ययम् ॥

Tadejati tannaijati, tad dure tat samipake; Tad antarasya sarvasya, tadu sarvasya baahyataha.

Ajo hamajaro ham cha, anaadini dhanah svayam; Avikaarash chidaananda, aniyaan mahato mahaan.

Apurvaanaam param nityam, svayam jyotir niraamayam; Virajam paramaakasham, dhruvam aananda mavyayam.

Thus the guru reveals: "I am unborn, I am ageless, beginningless and deathless. I am smaller than the smallest and larger than the largest. I move and move not.

I am far as well as near. I am inside everything and outside everything all at once. I am beyond cause and effect. I am the supreme akasha.

I am consciousness and bliss, never-ending, self-luminous, imperishable and pure."

55) चैतन्यं शाश्वतं शान्तं व्योमातीतं निरञ्जनम् ।
नादबिन्दुकलातीतं तस्मै श्रीगुरवे नमः ॥

Chaitanyam shaashvatam shaantam, vyomaatitam nirañjanam; Naada bindu kalaatitam, tasmai shri gurave namaha.

I bow to my guru, who is absolute consciousness, who is eternal, who is peace personified, who is completely pure, and who transcends the limits of space. He is beyond the primordial sound of nada. He is beyond the blue pearl, bindu. He is beyond the concentrated bliss of kala.

56) ज्ञानशक्तिसमारूढस् तत्त्वमालाविभूषितः ।
भुक्तिमुक्तिप्रदाता यस्तस्मै श्रीगुरवे नमः ॥

Jñaana shakti samaarudhas, tattva maalaa vibhushitaha; Bhukti mukti pradaataa yas, tasmai shri gurave namaha.

I bow to my guru, who is the embodiment of the jñana-shakti, the power of knowledge. The thirty-six tattvas are his garland. He bestows bhukti – worldly happiness, and mukti – spiritual awakening.

57) अनेकजन्मसम्प्राप्त - सर्वकर्म - विदाहिने।
स्वात्मज्ञानप्रभावेण तस्मै श्रीगुरवे नमः॥

Aneka janma sampraapta, sarva karma vidaahine;
Svaatma jñaana prabhaavena, tasmai shri gurave namaha.

I bow to my guru, who bestows atma-jñana, the knowledge of the Self. He burns away all the karmas carried forward from countless lifetimes.

58) न गुरोरधिकं तत्त्वं न गुरोरधिकं तपः।
तत्त्वं ज्ञानात्परं नास्ति तस्मै श्रीगुरवे नमः॥

Na guror adhikam tat tvam, na guror adhikam tapaha; Tat tvam jñaanaat param naasti, tasmai shri gurave namaha.

I bow to my guru, who embodies the great guru tattva, the universal principle of the guru, the highest truth and the greatest austerity. There is nothing worth knowing that is more important than this.

59) मन्नाथः श्रीजगन्नाथो मद्गुरुस्त्रिजगद्गुरुः।
ममात्मा सर्वभूतात्मा तस्मै श्रीगुरवे नमः॥

Mannaathah shri jagan naatho, madgurus trijagad guruhu; Mamaatmaa sarva bhutaatmaa, tasmai shri gurave namaha.

My guru is the Lord of the universe. My guru is the guru of the three worlds. My Self is the universal Atman. To my guru, I bow.

60) गुरुरादिरनादिश्च गुरुः परम-दैवतम्।
गुरोः परतरं नास्ति तस्मै श्रीगुरवे नमः।

Gurur aadir anaadhish cha, guruh parama daivatam; Guroh parataram naasti, tasmai shri gurave namaha.

The guru, the first impulse of creation, is eternal and without end. He is without question the supreme of all deities. Nothing exists which is greater than he. To my Sadguru, I bow.

61

यस्य स्मरणमात्रेण ज्ञानमुत्पद्यते स्वयम् ।
य एव सर्वसम्प्राप्तिस्तस्मै श्रीगुरवे नमः ।
एवंविधं गुरुं ध्यात्वा ज्ञानमुत्पद्यते स्वयम् ।
तत्सद्गुरुप्रसादेन मुक्तोऽहमिति भावयेत् ॥

Yasya smarana maatrena, jñaanam utpadyate svayam; Ya eva sarva sampraaptis, tasmai shri gurave namaha.

Evam vidham gurum dhyaatvaa, jñaanam utpadyate svayam; Tat sadguru prasaadena, mukto hamiti bhaavayet.

Merely recalling my guru, knowledge arises spontaneously. Remembering him brings all attainments automatically.

By meditating on the guru in this way, the prasad of my guru's grace delivers me to realization.

62)

ब्रह्मानन्दं परमसुखदं केवलं ज्ञानमूर्तिं
द्वन्द्वातीतं गगनसदृशं तत्त्वमस्यादिलक्ष्यम् ।
एकं नित्यं विमलमचलं सर्वधीसाक्षिभूतं
भावातीतं त्रिगुणरहितं सद्गुरुं तं नमामि ।
नित्यं शुद्धं निराभासं निराकारं निरञ्जनम् ।
नित्यबोधं चिदानन्दं गुरुं ब्रह्म नमाम्यहम् ॥

Brahmaanandam parama sukhadam, kevalam jñaana murtim, dvandvaatitam gagana sadrsham, tat tvam asyaadi lakshyam; Ekam nityam vimalam achalam, sarvadhi saakshi bhutam, bhaavaatitam triguna rahitam, sad gurum tam namaami. Nityam shuddham niraabhaasam, niraakaaram nirañjanam; Nitya bodham chidaanandam, gurum brahma namaamyaham.

i bow to my guru who is the infinite ocean of consciousness, beyond perception, beyond duality, beyond the three gunas and all formation. he is the embodiment of the bliss of brahman and the bestower of ultimate happiness. he is ekam - one; he is nityam - eternal; he is vimalam - free from impurities; he is achalam - steadfast. he is the abode of knowledge and bliss, and is forever omniscient, omnipresent and vast like the sky. he is the witness. to realize the great vedantic mahavakya "Tat Tvam asi", "Thou art that", is to become one with the guru.

63

स्फटिकप्रतिमारूपं दृश्यते दर्पणे यथा।
तथात्मनि चिदाकारमानन्दं सोऽहमित्युत॥

Sphatika pratimaa rupam, drshyate darpane yathaa; Tathaatmani chidaakaaram, aanandam so hamityuta.

Just as a crystal reflected in a mirror, replicates its shining image, in the same way, when the infinite ocean of consciousness is seen in the atman, the bliss of realization dawns and the awareness of soham arises – "I am that".

64

ज्ञानं विज्ञानसहितं लभ्यते गुरुभक्तितः।
गुरोः परतरं नास्ति ध्येयोऽसौ गुरुमार्गिभिः॥

Jñaanam vijñaana sahitam, labhyate guru bhaktitaha; Guroh parataram naasti, dhyeyo sau guru maargibhihi.

By following the guru margena, the path of the guru, and meditating upon him, one obtains jnana – knowledge, as well as vijñana – insight. There is nothing greater than the guru.

65) गुरुदर्शित-मार्गेण मनःशुद्धिं तु कारयेत् ।
अनित्यं खण्डयेत्सर्वं यत्किञ्चिदात्मगोचरम् ॥

Guru darshita maargena, manah shuddhim tu kaarayet; Anityam khandayet sarvam, yatkiñchid aatma gocharam.

by following the guru's path, one's mind becomes purified. thus one is then able to detach from the transitory objects of the world, and be free from the binding influence of false identification.

66) गुरोः कृपाप्रसादेन आत्मारामं निरीक्षयेत् ।
अनेन गुरुमार्गेण स्वात्मज्ञानं प्रवर्तते ॥

Guroh krpaa prasaadena, atmaaraamam nirikshayet; Anena guru maargena, svattma jñaanam pravartate.

by following the guru margena, one attains the highest goal – the realization of the bliss of ātman. this is generated through prasad, the gift of the guru's grace.

67) श्रीमत्परब्रह्म गुरुं स्मरामि श्रीमत्परब्रह्म गुरुं वदामि ।
श्रीमत्परब्रह्म गुरुं नमामि श्रीमत्परब्रह्म गुरुं भजामि ॥

Shrimat parabrahma gurum smaraami,
Shrimat parabrahma gurum vadaami,
Shrimat parabrahma gurum namaami,
Shrimat parabrahma gurum bhajaami.

I remember my Shri Guru, who is the supreme brahman.

I speak of my Shri Guru, who is the supreme brahman.

I bow to my Shri Guru, who is the supreme brahman.

I worship my Shri Guru, who is the supreme brahman.

68) आनन्दमानन्दकरं प्रसन्नं ज्ञानस्वरूपं ।
निजबोधयुक्तम् योगीन्द्रमीड्यं भवरोग ।
वैद्यं श्रीमद्गुरुं नित्यमहं नमामि ॥

Aananda maananda karam prasannam, jñaana svarupam nijabodha yuktam; Yogindra midyam bhava roga vaidyam, shrimad gurum nitya maham namaami.

To the eternal Shri guru I bow. he is bliss incarnate, exuding joy. his countenance radiates ecstasy. he is awake with knowledge of his own Self. the yogis worship him as their lord. With the precision of a surgeon, he extricates us from the wheel of cyclic existence.

69) यस्मिन्सृष्टिस्थितिध्वंस निग्रहानुग्रहात्मकम् ।
कृत्यं पञ्चविधं शश्वद्भासते तं नमाम्यहम् ॥

Yasmin srshti sthiti dhvamsa, nigrahaanugrahaat makam; Krtyam pañcha vidham shaashvad, bhaasate tam namaamyaham.

I bow to the guru, who embodies lord bhairava, constantly revealing the five functions of creation, maintenance, dissolution, concealment and the bestowal of grace.

70) एवं श्रुत्वा महादेवि गुरुनिन्दां करोति यः।
स याति नरकं घोरं यावच्चन्द्रदिवाकरौ।
यावत्कल्पान्तको देहस्तावदेव गुरुं स्मरेत्।
गुरुलोपो न कर्तव्यः स्वच्छन्दो यदि वा भवेत्।
हुंकारेण न वक्तव्यं प्राज्ञैः शिष्यैः कथञ्चन।
गुरोरग्रे न वक्तव्यमसत्यं च कदाचन॥

Evam shrutvaa mahaadevi, guru nindaam karoti yah; Sa yaati narakam ghoram, yaavach chandra divaakarau. Yaavat kalpaantako dehas, taavadeva gurum smaret; Guru lopo na kartavyah, svachchando yadi vaa bhavet. Hunkaarena na vaktavyam, praajñaih shishyaih kathañchana; Guror agre na vaktavyam, asatyam cha kadaachana.

O great goddess, one's behavior with the guru is of utmost importance. One should never behave egotistically before the guru. Never tell a lie to the guru or speak discourteously to him. Never speak ill of the guru or forsake him, even if you don't understand his actions. Remember the guru for all eternity. If you ignore this teaching, in spite of hearing it, you will risk a most dreadful fate, which will last as long as the sun and moon both shine.

71) श्रुतिस्मृति अविज्ञाय केवलं गुरुसेवकाः।
ते वै सन्न्यासिनः प्रोक्ता इतरे वेषधारिणः॥

Shruti smrti avijñaaya, kevalam guru sevakaaha; Te vai sannyaasinah proktaa, itare vesha dhaarinaha.

It is not the knowledge of ancient scriptures, such as the Vedas and Smritis, nor is the wearing of the clothing of a monk, that makes a true seeker. A genuine sadhu is a servant and disciple of his guru.

72) नित्यं ब्रह्म निराकारं निर्गुणं बोधयेत्परम्।
सर्वं ब्रह्म निराभासं दीपो दीपान्तरं यथा॥

Nityam brahma niraakaaram, nirgunam bodhayet param; Sarvam brahma niraabhaasam, dipo dipaantaram yathaa.

Through the mystery of Shaktipat, the light of the guru kindles the light within his disciple, just as one candle is used to light another candle. The descent of grace opens the way for the disciple to realize that everything is the ocean of Consciousness, which is beyond the perception of the senses, omnipresent, eternal, beyond imputed terms and without form.

73)

गुरुध्यानं तथा कृत्वा स्वयं ब्रह्ममयो भवेत् ।
पिण्डे पदे तथा रूपे मुक्तोऽसौ नात्र संशयः ॥

Guru dhyaanam tathaa krtvaa, svayam brahma mayo bhavet; Pinde pade tathaa rupe, mukto sau naatra samshayah.

A disciple becomes one with brahman by meditating on the guru. In this way, the stages of samadhi undoubtedly unfold – pinda, pada and rupa.

74)

श्रीपार्वत्युवाच
पिण्डं किं तु महादेव पदं किं समुदाहृतम् ।
रूपातीतं च रूपं किं एतदाख्याहि शङ्कर ॥

Shri Paarvati-uvaacha:
Pindam kim tu mahaadeva, padam kim samudaahrtam; Rupaatitam cha rupam kim, etadaakhyaahi shankara.

Parvati asked:
O lord Shankara, please explain these terms to me – what are pinda, pada and rupa? And is there more beyond them?

75) श्रीमहादेव उवाच
पिण्डं कुण्डलिनीशक्तिः पदं हंसमुदाहृतम् ।
रूपं बिन्दुरिति ज्ञेयं रूपातीतं निरञ्जनम् ॥

Shri Mahaadeva uvaacha: Pindam kundalini shaktih, padam hamsa mudaah rtam; Rupam binduriti jñeyam, rupaatitam nirañjanam.

Lord Shiva answered:
Kundalini Shakti is pinda, the attainment of Shaktipat. Hamsa is pada, when the awareness of Soham becomes unbroken. Bindu is rupa, the enduring vision of the blue pearl. And there is also rupatita, beyond rupa, known as niranjanam – merging with pure being.

76) पिण्डे मुक्ता पदे मुक्ता रूपे मुक्ता वरानने ।
रूपातीते तु ये मुक्तास्ते मुक्ता नात्र संशयः ॥

Pinde muktaa pade muktaa, rupe muktaa varaanane; Rupaatite tu ye muktaas, te muktaa naatra samshayaha.

O my beautiful one, pinda, pada and rupa are each a specific landmark on the path of liberation, but the highest liberation is found in rupatitam, that transcendental awareness of pure Consciousness.

77) अगोचरं तथाऽगम्यं नामरूपविवर्जितम् ।
निःशब्दं तद्विजानीयात् स्वभावं ब्रह्म पार्वति ॥

Agocharam tathaa gamyam, naama rupa vivar jitam; Nihshabdam tad vijaaniyaat, svabhaavam brahma paarvati.

Goddess Parvati, know brahman, the supreme reality, the great void. It is without quality, without form, without name, without sound and beyond perception and understanding.

78) स्वयं सर्वमयो भूत्वा परं तत्त्वं विलोकयेत् ।
परात्परतरं नान्यत् सर्वमेतन्निरालयम् ॥

Svayam sarva mayo bhutvaa, param tat tvam vilokayet; Paraat parataram naanyat, sarvametan niraalayam.

Merge into unity with pure Consciousness and attain oneness with all. As you find everything arising simultaneously within you, you realize only this supreme principle alone exists.

79) समुद्रे च यथा तोयं क्षीरे क्षीरं घृते घृतम् ।
भिन्ने कुम्भे यथाकाशस्तथात्मा परमात्मनि ॥

Samudre cha yathaa toyam, kshire kshiram
ghrte ghrtam; Bhinne kumbhe yathaa kaashas,
tathaatmaa paramaatmani.

The way the individual soul merges into universal consciousness is like the water of many rivers merging into the ocean, or like the space inside and outside a clay pot finally being perceived as the same space.

80) सर्वज्ञ-पदमित्याहुर्देही सर्वमयो बुधाः ।
सदानन्दः सदा शान्तो रमते यत्र कुत्रचित् ।
तथैव ज्ञानी जीवात्मा परमात्मनि लीयते ।
ऐक्येन रमते ज्ञानी यत्र तत्र दिवानिशम् ॥

Sarvajña padam ityaahur, dehi sarva mayo budhaha;
Sadaananda sadaa shaanto, ramate yatra kutra chit.
Tathaiva jñaani jivaatmaa, paramaatmani liyate;
Aikyena ramate jñaani, yatra tatra divaanisham.

This is the state of realization, when the individual embodied soul merges into the supreme Self. Having established unity consciousness, he celebrates this oneness day and night, always blissful, always tranquil, wherever he may be.

81) तस्यावलोकनं प्राप्य सर्वसङ्गविवर्जितः ।
एकाकी निःस्पृहः शान्तस्तिष्ठासेत् तत्प्रसादतः ॥

Tasyaa valokanam praapya, sarva sanga vivarjitaha; Ekaaki nishpriha shaantas, tishthaaset tat prasaadataha.

After attaining this solitary and tranquil state, through the grace of the guru, all your attachments and desires dissolve into nothing.

82) स एव च गुरुः साक्षात् सदा सद्ब्रह्मवित्तमः ।
तस्य स्थानानि सर्वाणि पवित्राणि न संशयः ॥

Sa eva cha guruh saakshaat, sadaa sadbrahma vittamaha; Tasya staanaani sarvaani, pavitraani na samshayaha.

He who attains the realization of brahman, the highest knowledge, indeed becomes the guru. Then, without a doubt, wherever he goes, he experiences the divine.

83) एवंविधो महामुक्तः सर्वदा वर्तते बुधः।
तस्य सर्वप्रयत्नेन भावभक्तिं करोति यः॥

Evam vidho mahaamuktah, sarvadaa vartate budhaha; Tasya sarva prayatnena, bhaava bhaktim karoti yah.

Then the life of a fully liberated person of wisdom becomes filled with devotion. He focuses his every effort on service to God.

84) सर्वसन्देहरहितो मुक्तो भवति पार्वति।
भुक्तिमुक्तिद्वयं तस्य जिह्वाग्रे च सरस्वती॥

Sarva sandeha rahito, mukto bhavati paarvati; Bhukti mukti dvayam tasya, jihvaagre cha sarasvati.

He is free from worries, and bhukti and mukti are his to enjoy – worldly fulfillment and liberation. O Parvati, his tongue is graced with Saraswati, the goddess of speech, learning and knowledge.

85) यत्रैव तिष्ठते सोऽपि स देशः पुण्यभाजनम् ।
मुक्तस्य लक्षणं देवि तवाग्रे कथितं मया ॥
सर्वशुद्धः पवित्रोऽसौ स्वभावाद्यत्र तिष्ठति ।
तत्र देवगणाः सर्वे क्षेत्रे पीठे वसन्ति हि ।

Yatraiva tishthate so pi, sa deshah punya bhaajanam; Muktasya lakshanam devi, tavaagre kathitam mayaa.

Sarva shuddhah pavitro sau, svabhaavaad yatra tishthati; Tatra deva ganaah sarve, kshetre pithe vasanti hi.

The supreme purity and taintless quality of the guru draw all that is holy to him – so the place where he lives naturally becomes sanctified and filled with a multitude of deities.

In these ways, O goddess, I have described the nature of a liberated person to you.

86)

उपदेशस्तथा देवि गुरुमार्गेण मुक्तिदः ।
गुरुभक्तिस्तथा ध्यानं सकलं तव कीर्तितम् ॥

Upadeshas tathaa devi, guru maargena muktidaha;
Guru bhaktis tathaa dhyaanam, sakalam tava kirtitam.

O devi, by following the path of the guru, I have clearly shown you how to achieve this liberation through devotion to the guru and through meditation on the guru.

87)

अनेन यद्भवेत्कार्यं तद्वदामि महामते ।
लोकोपकारकं देवि लौकिकं तु न भावयेत् ॥

Anena yad bhavet kaaryam, tad vadaami mahaamate; Loko pakaarakam devi, laukikam tu na bhaavayet.

O wise one, much can be accomplished through these spiritual practices. Focus your attention on service and working for the welfare of people, instead of using your accrued shakti for self-centered worldly gain.

88)

लौकिकात्कर्मणो यान्ति ज्ञानहीना भवार्णवम् ।
ज्ञानी तु भावयेत्सर्वं कर्म निष्कर्म यत्कृतम् ॥

Laukikaat karmano yaanti, jñaana hinaa bhavaarnavam; Jñaani tu bhaavayet sarvam, karma nishkarma yatkrtam.

Without knowledge of brahman, all your actions are worldly and continue to spool on more and more karma, sinking you further into the ocean of samsara. A knower of truth has unspooled all his karma, and all his subsequent actions are no longer binding and collect no further karma.

89)

गुरुगीतात्मकं देवि शुद्धतत्त्वं मयोदितम् ।
भवव्याधिविनाशार्थं स्वयमेव जपेत्सदा ॥

Guru gitaat makam devi, shuddha tat tvam mayoditam; Bhava vyaadi vinaashaartham, svayam eva japet sadaa.

O devi, this truth which I have revealed to you takes the form of the guru gita. Repeat it often to remove the binding influence of the wheel of cyclic existence.

90) इदं तु भक्तिभावेन पठते शृणुते यदि।
लिखित्वा तत्प्रदातव्यं तत्सर्वं सफलं भवेत्॥

Idam tu bhakti bhaavena, pathate shrunute yadi;
Likhitvaa tat pradaatavyam, tat sarvam saphalam bhavet.

Contemplate this guru gita with devotion – read it, listen to the guru recite it, journal about it. This will yield the fruit of liberation.

91) गुरुगीताक्षरैकं तु मन्त्रराजमिमं जपेत्।
अन्ये च विविधा मन्त्राः कलां नार्हन्ति षोडशीम्॥

Guru gitaak sharaikam tu, mantra raajam imam japet; Anye cha vividhaa mantraah, kalaam naarhanti shodashim.

Recite the guru gita. Each and every letter is an empowered mantra. Other mantras do not have the merit of even one-sixteenth part of it.

92

अनन्तफलमाप्नोति गुरुगीताजपेन तु ।
सर्वपापप्रशमनं सर्वदारिद्र्यनाशनम् ॥

Ananta phalam aapnoti, guru gitaa japena tu; Sarva paapa prashamanam, sarva daaridrya naashanam.

bountiful rewards are obtained by repeating the guru gita. the recitation removes all obstacles and ends all suffering and hardship.

93

कालमृत्युभयहरं सर्वसङ्कटनाशनम् ।
यक्षराक्षसभूतानां चोरव्याघ्रभयापहम् ॥

Kaala mrtyu bhaya haram, sarva sankata naashanam; Yaksha raakshasa bhutaanaam, chora vyaaghra bhayaapaham.

it removes the fear of time and death, and is the destroyer of all adversity, while protecting one from the influence of wild spirits, demons, ghosts and thieves.

94) महाव्याधिहरं सर्व विभूतिसिद्धिदं भवेत् ।
अथवा मोहनं वश्यं स्वयमेव जपेत्सदा ॥

Mahaa vyaadhi haram sarvam, vibhuti siddhidam bhavet; Athavaa mohanam vashyam, svayam eva japet sadaa.

It removes the disease of worldly existence. It bestows riches and siddhis, as well as the ability to influence others. Always repeat the Guru Gita.

95) मोहनं सर्वभूतानां बन्धमोक्षकरं भवेत् ।
देवराजप्रियकरं सर्वलोकवशं भवेत् ॥

Mohanam sarva bhutaanaam, bandha moksha karam bhavet; Deva raaja priya karam, sarva loka vasham bhavet.

Through this repetition, one becomes free from bondage, gains the favor of all the gods and attains lordship of the deities of Consciousness.

96) सर्वेषां स्तम्भनकरं गुणानां च विवर्धनम् ।
दुष्कर्म-नाशनं चैव सुकर्मसिद्धिदं भवेत् ॥

Sarveshaam stambhana karam, gunaanaam cha vivardhanam; Dushkarma naashanam chaiva, sukarma siddhidam bhavet.

The Guru Gita brings one into direct contact with the pillar of the Siddha lineage. It brings the refined, spiritual qualities of sattva guna to the forefront. It increases good karma and dissolves bad karma.

97) असिद्धं साधयेत् कार्यं नवग्रहभयापहम् ।
दुःस्वप्न-नाशनं चैव सुस्वप्न-फलदायकम् ॥

Asiddham saadhayet kaaryam, navagraha bhayaapaham; Duhsvapna naashanam chaiva, susvapna phala daayakam.

Repeating the Guru Gita aligns one's life with the Guru. It brings good dreams to fruition and curtails bad dreams. Fear of the astrological influence of the nine planets is diminished; and unfinished tasks become easy to complete.

98) सर्व-बाधा-प्रशमनं धर्मार्थ-काम-मोक्षदम् ।
यं यं चिन्तयते कामं तं तं प्राप्नोति निश्चितम् ॥

Sarva baadhaa prashamanam, dharmaartha kaama moksha dam; Yam yam chintayate kaamaam, tam tam praapnoti nishchitam.

It removes all obstacles and quickens the fulfillment of desires. It accomplishes the four-fold goals of life:

> dharma – righteous duty;
> artha – wealth;
> kama – pleasure;
> moksha – liberation.

99) मोक्षहेतुर्जपेन्नित्यं मोक्षश्रियमवाप्नुयात् ।
भोगकामो जपेद्यो वै तस्य कामफलप्रदम् ॥

Moksha hetur japen nityam, moksha shriyam avaapnuyaat; Bhoga kaamo japed yo vai, tasya kaama phala pradam.

If one's goal is liberation, the Guru Gita should be recited regularly. The glory of liberation will be attained, as well as the fruition of worldly desire.

100) संसारमल-नाशार्थं भवपाशनिवृत्तये ।
गुरुगीताम्भसि स्नानं तत्त्वज्ञः कुरुते सदा ॥

Samsaara mala naashaartham, bhava paasha nivrttaye; Guru gitaam bhasi snaanam, tat tvajñah kurute sadaa.

Repeat the Guru Gita and bathe in the cleansing waters of the ocean of truth, thus washing away the impurities of the world and the binding trap of samsara, the cycle of birth and death.

101) अथ काम्यजपे स्थानं कथयामि वरानने।
सागरे वा सरित्तीरेऽथवा हरिहरालये।
शक्तिदेवालये गोष्ठे सर्वदेवालये शुभे।
वटे च धात्रीमूले वा मठे वृन्दावने तथा।
पवित्रे निर्मले स्थाने नित्यानुष्ठानतोऽपि वा।
निर्वेदनेन मौनेन जपमेतं समाचरेत्।
श्मशाने भयभूमौ तु वटमूलान्तिके तथा।
सिध्यन्ति धौत्तरे मूले चूतवृक्षस्य सन्निधौ॥

Atha kaamya jape sthaanam, katha yaami varaanane; Saagare vaa sarittire, thavaa hari haraalaye. Shakti devaalaye goshte, sarva devaalaye shubhe; Vate cha dhaatri mule vaa, mate vrndaavane tathaa. Pavitre nirmale sthaane, nityaa nushthaanato pi vaa; Nirvedanena maunena, japam etam samaacharet. Smashaane bhaya bhumau tu, vata mulaantike tathaa; Siddhyanti dhauttare mule, chuta vrkshasya sannidhau.

having established inner silence of the mind, repeat the guru gita with detachment, in a clean and sacred place. now i shall speak of the places that are beneficial for this spiritual practice: at the seashore, along a river, in all holy temples and shrines such as those to shiva, shakti or vishnu, in a cowshed, by sacred trees, such as the dhatri or mango, thorn-apple or banyan, in a grove of tulsi plants, or in an ashram. O beautiful one, it is also fruitful to repeat the guru gita in a cemetery or in frightening desolate places.

102

वस्त्रासने च दारिद्र्यं पाषाणे रोगसंभवः।
मेदिन्यां दुःखमाप्नोति काष्ठे भवति निष्फलम्।
कृष्णाजिने ज्ञानसिद्धिर्मोक्षश्रीर्व्याघ्रचर्मणि।
कुशासने ज्ञानसिद्धिः सर्वसिद्धिस्तु कम्बले॥

Vastraasane cha daaridryam, paashaane roga sambhavaha; Medinyaam duhkham aapnoti, kaashthe bhavati nishphalam. Krshnaajine jñaana siddhir, mokshashrir vyaghra charmani; Kushaasane jñaana siddhih, sarva siddhistu kambale.

O devi, prepare your seat well, with the proper asana. Use a white woolen blanket placed over kusha or durva grass, to reap the highest attainments. Or use a tiger skin or black deer skin, which give rise to liberation and knowledge. Other seats are not as favorable for your practice, such as cloth, wood or sitting directly on the ground.

103) कुशैर्वा दूर्वया देवि आसने शुभ्रकम्बले ।
उपविश्य ततो देवि जपेदेकाग्रमानसः ।
ध्येयं शुक्लं च शान्त्यर्थं वश्ये रक्तासनं प्रिये ।
अभिचारे कृष्णवर्णं पीतवर्णं धनागमे ॥

Kushairvaa durvayaa devi, aasane shubhra kambale; Upavishya tato devi, japed ekaagra maanasaha. Dhyeyam shuklam cha shaantyartham, vashye raktaasanam priye; Abhichaare krshna varnam, pita varnam dhanaa game.

how you position your seat is also important. To influence others, sit on a red seat facing east. To defeat demons, sit on a black seat facing south. To gain wealth, sit on a yellow seat facing west. but the highest outcome is achieved when you recite the guru gita facing north on a white seat, and realize peace.

104) सत्यं सत्यं पुनः सत्यं धर्म्यं साङ्ख्यं मयोदितम् ।
गुरुगीतासमं नास्ति सत्यं सत्यं वरानने ॥

Satyam saytam punah satyam, dharmyam saankhyam mayo ditam; Gurugitaa samam naasti, satyam satyam varaanane.

Satyam. Satyam. The guru gita is the truth. There is nothing else like it, O beautiful one. I have revealed this truth to you in answer to your longing. This is the truth. This is the truth.

105) माता धन्या पिता धन्यो धन्यो वंशः कुलं तथा। धन्या च वसुधा देवि गुरुभक्तिः सुदुर्लभा॥

Maataa dhanyaa pitaa dhanyo, dhanyo vamshah kulam tathaa; Dhanyaa cha vasudhaa devi, guru bhaktih sudurlabhaa.

O goddess, the dedication of one's life to the guru is extraordinary. Everything is affected by this devotion – the devotee's mother, father, family and ancestry are all blessed. Even the earth itself rejoices.

106) गुरुभावः परं तीर्थमन्यतीर्थं निरर्थकम् ।
सर्वतीर्थाश्रयं देवि पादाङ्गुष्ठं च वर्तते ॥

Guru bhaavah param tirtham, anya tirtham nirarthakam; Sarva tirthaash rayam devi, paadaan gustham cha vartate.

Complete immersion in the guru – gurubhava – is the most holy pilgrimage. Going to any other place of pilgrimage is hollow and futile. O Parvati, why go somewhere else to worship, when the big toe of the guru's foot is the ultimate abode of all that is sacred.

107) न गुरोरधिकं न गुरोरधिकं
न गुरोरधिकं न गुरोरधिकम् ।
शिवशासनतः शिवशासनतः
शिवशासनतः शिवशासनतः ॥

Na guror adhikam, na guror adhikam, na guror adhikam, na guror adhikam;
Shiva shaasanatah, shiva shaasanatah, shiva shaasanatah, shiva shaasanataha.

beyond the guru there is nothing. beyond the guru there is nothing. beyond the guru there is nothing. beyond the guru there is nothing.

This is the word of Shiva. This is the word of Shiva. This is the word of Shiva. This is the word of Shiva.

108) इदमेव शिवं त्विदमेव शिवं त्विदमेव शिवं त्विदमेव शिवम् ।
मम शासनतो मम शासनतो
मम शासनतो मम शासनतः ॥

Idameva shivam tvidameva shivam, tvidameva shivam tvidameva shivam;
Mama shaasanato mama shaasanato, mama shaasanato mama shaasanataha.

Indeed, the guru gita is Shiva. The guru gita is Shiva. The guru gita is Shiva. The guru gita is indeed Shiva.

This is my supreme command. This is my supreme command. This is my supreme command. This is my supreme command.

इति श्रीस्कन्दपुराणे उत्तरखण्डे ईश्वरपार्वतीसंवादे
गुरुगीता समाप्ता ।

श्रीगुरुदेवचरणार्पणमस्तु ॥

Iti shri skanda puraane, uttara khande ishvara paarvati samvaade, Gurugitaa samaaptaa, Shri gurudeva charanaar panamastu

And so ends the guru gita - the discourse given by lord Shiva to his consort, the goddess Parvati, and recorded in the text of the Shri Skanda Purana.

I offer this guru gita at the revered lotus feet of my guru.

Pronunciation Guide for Sanskrit Transliteration

There are no exact matches for several Sanskrit sounds in English, so some approximations have been given. Use this guide to help you with the proper pronunciation of the Guru Gita in Sanskrit, as you read the transliteration below the Devanagari Sanskrit text on the preceding pages.

One of the greatest differences between Sanskrit and English is the pronunciation of vowel sounds. English has only one variety of a, e, i, o, u – and it is through experience that we know they are pronounced differently depending on the word they are found in.

In contrast, Sanskrit has sixteen vowels, including two **a** sounds, two **i** sounds and two **u** sounds, etc. The difference between one and the other is only whether it is short or long.

The vowel that is the most important for a Westerner to understand is **a**. To differentiate it, we have shown the short **a** as a single a, and the long **a** as a double aa.

To the Westerner, the difference between the short and long e, i, u and o sounds are not so strongly different. For strict pronunciation, the difference is simply how long the sound is held. This is a subtlety we have decided not to emphasize in this translation, so we have shown these vowels as though they are the same, regardless of whether they are short or long.

a ~ pronounced like a short u, like d**u**h, b**u**t

aa ~ pronounced with a long a, as in **aw**l, l**aw**, s**aw**, **a**rm, h**a**rm

i ~ pronounced like t**ee**, s**ee**

u ~ pronounced like b**oo**, wh**o**, what's n**ew**?

e ~ pronounced like h**ay**, ok**ay**

o ~ pronounced like **oh** n**o**!

r ~ in Sanskrit, there is an 'r' sound that is actually a vowel. When you see an 'r' before another consonant (ex: krtam), give the 'r' a little roll of the tongue to lead it into the letters that follow. Sometimes it helps to imagine an invisible short 'i' after the 'r' sound, to help you say it.

There are a couple Sanskrit vowels that are diphthongs;their sound changes from the back of the mouth to the front of the mouth:

ai ~ pronounced like "I", f**i**ght, p**ie**, **ai**sle

au ~ pronounced like **ow**, h**ow**, c**ow**, h**ou**nd

ha/hi/hu ~ at the end of many Sanskrit words or phrases, you often see what looks like a colon ":" in the Devanagari. This is known as visarga. Pronounce this as though there were a faint repeat or echo of the vowel that precedes it. We have transliterated it as a 'ha', 'hi' or 'hu'. When you find the 'ha' or 'hi' at the end of a word, remember to pronounce it gently, almost breathlessly.

th ~ this is a real trick for the Westerner, because when we see a *t* and an *h* together, we always want to pronounce it like *th*is or *th*at. In Sanskrit, there is no '*th*' sound like that. The way to pronounce it is like a **t** with air coming after it, like the word 'an**th**ill'. As an example, in verse 98, the word for wealth is *artha*, and is pronounced more like arta. Technically, it is a **t** sound with air or aspiration after it, as though you were saying "art (h)a", making the 'ha' sound very gentle and soft.

ph ~ this is something else to watch for, because

when we see a *p* and an *h* together, we always want to pronounce it with the sound of *f*, like fit. In Sanskrit, there is no '*f*' sound like that. The way to pronounce it is like a **p** with air coming after it, like the word '**po**wer' or '**po**und'. As an example, in verse 8, the word *phalam* is pronounced more like palam. Technically, it is a **p** sound with air or aspiration after it, as though you were saying "p (h)alam", making the 'ha' sound very gentle and soft.

kh, gh, jh, dh, bh ~ similar to 'th' and 'ph' above, these consonant combinations mean there is a slight aspiration, as though you have extra air following the pronunciation of each consonant. For instance, gh is pronounced like 'do**gh**ouse'; rh is pronounced like 'roa**dh**ouse'; bh is pronounced like 'a**bh**or', etc.

ñ ~ pronounced like 'nya'

jñ ~ there are several correct ways to say this. It's acceptable to pronounce it like 'gnya' or as 'jnya', or even better yet, somewhere between 'gnya' and 'jnya'.

GLOSSARY

A – Ka – Tha ~ Within the cerebrum of the brain are many aspects of the subtle body. The triangle referred to in the Guru Gita is a formation that is in the physical brain as well as the subtle body. Inside this triangle is absolute void, infinite black consciousness, without form and without quality. This triangle is located in the center of the Brahmarandhra and is formed by the Sanskrit alphabet. Each of the letters of the Sanskrit alphabet are understood to be sacred mantras. The first letter of the alphabet is "A" (pronounced ah). It and the next 15 letters form the first side of the triangle. The next set of letters beginning with "Ka" form the second side of the triangle and the last set of letters beginning with "Tha" (pronounced ta) form the third side. A, Ka and Tha are at each of the three points. The Guru's two lotus feet, which are Ham and Sa are in the center of this sacred triangle.

Akasha ~ ("not visible") Space, ether or sky. It is the fifth element along with the other four elements of earth (prithivi), air (vayu), fire (agni) and water (apa). It is also the most subtle element. It permeates all dimensions and represents all spaces – the inner, outer, physical and spiritual.

Asana ~ ("seat") The name for the cloth or skin that one sits on for meditation. By using the same asana over and over, it is thought that the vibrations of the meditation permeate the cloth and accumulate, thereby enhancing the experience. Shiva is usually pictured sitting on a tiger skin, which symbolizes lust. He thus shows his complete control over all passion.

Atman ~ (from the Sanskrit root at = "to breathe") The transcendental Self or Spirit. It is the eternal, superconscious, Supreme Soul, and Divine Self within each individual. The spiritual essence of all individual human beings.

Bhairava ~ The fierce manifestation of Shiva that is associated with the simultaneous expression of creation, maintenance, dissolution, concealment and the bestowal of grace. (see Five Acts)

Bhukti ~ Worldly fulfillment and enjoyment, acknowledged to be an important component of a balanced life.

Blue Pearl ~ A scintillating blue light or bindu,

the size of a tiny seed that can appear during meditation. It is said to be the doorway to the inner Self and contains the entire universe.

Bodhicitta ~ ("the essence of enlightenment") Formed by the heart/mind connection, it represents the union of formation and emptiness. Bodhicitta reflects the truth of enlightenment, which does not come from an outside agency, but comes from within you as you. Alignment with the Bodhicitta produces an irresistible force for awakening.

Brahma ~ One of the three gods of the Hindu trinity: Brahma (the Creator of the Universe), Vishnu (the Preserver) and Shiva (the Destroyer). He is often depicted with four heads, four faces and four arms, representing the four directions of east, west, north and south. He continually recites the four Vedas with each of his four heads. (see Vedas)

Brahman ~ (from the root brh = "to expand, greater than the greatest") The supreme all-pervading spiritual essence of the universe. Known in Vedic philosophy as Absolute Consciousness. The ultimate reality that is the principle behind the origin of the universe and of the gods. Brahman is THAT, the all inclusive. Described as sat-chit-ananda: being-consciousness-bliss.

Brahmarandra ~ ("the hole of Brahman") Located in the thousand-petaled chakra at the crown of the head, it is the soft spot at the brain found in infants; the point where the infusion of life takes place in the human being. It is just underneath the skull embedded in the upper layer of the cerebrum, which is the part of the brain that is dedicated to the highest brain functions. This is also the seat of the Guru. It is the superior place to exit the body upon death. (See the concept of "phowa" in The Bardo Thodol by Mark Griffin).

Causal Body ~ Refers to one of the four bodies: physical, subtle physical, causal and supra causal. It is a body without physical form. It is mind itself and encompasses the mental faculties of manas (mind), buddhi (intellect), ahamkara (ego) and infinitely more levels that become revealed upon awakening.

Devanagari ~ (from the Sanskrit roots deva = "gods" + naagari = "city") the Sanskrit alphabet; literally, the city of the Gods or the writing of the Gods.

Devi ~ (from the Sanskrit root div = "to shine") Goddess, the embodiment of female energy and the universal great divine mother, who is Shakti.

Represented in the Guru Gita in her benign aspect as Parvati, the beloved of Shiva. The fierce aspect of the Goddess is Kali or Durga, though any manifestation of the Goddess is known as devi, which is the feminine word for God. Deva is the masculine word for God and is used in the Sanskrit version of the Guru Gita when referring to Shiva.

Dharma ~ (from the Sanskrit root dhr = "to uphold, to sustain, to carry") That which supports or sustains the universe. The ultimate law, the essential duty, the righteous way. To say that one performs one's dharma means that one is acting from total alignment with one's own life's highest purpose. It is the basic principle of divine law and the basis of all social and moral order.

Duality ~ The understanding that the universe is composed of binary oppositions, such as male and female, light and dark, good and evil, etc. It often refers to the opposition of Self and other, or form and emptiness. The Upanishads say, "Fear is born from duality". In the Guru Gita, when it is said that the Guru is beyond duality, it means that the Guru, because he lives in unity consciousness – Nirvikalpa Samadhi – knows that state of awareness that perceives all phenomenon as manifesting simultaneously.

Emptiness ~ Mentioned in the Guru Gita as a state which is beyond all imputed terms (see imputed terms below). It has nothing to do with an empty or lonely feeling or an empty glass of water. It is the state of void, containing nothing and yet containing everything. There is nothing similar to it and nothing different from it.

Five Acts ~ (In Sanskrit, pañchakritya = "five fold activity") Creation, maintenance, concealment, destruction and the bestowal of grace. The often seen statue of Shiva Nataraj symbolizes these five acts. In this statue Shiva is shown having four arms. His right hand holds a small drum, where the sound of creation is born. His other right hand is raised in the traditional mudra or position granting protection, which represents sustenance in his function as the maintainer. His left hand holds fire, which symbolizes destruction. His other left hand turns inward, shielding, signifying concealment. His raised left foot signifies the bestowal of grace. His balanced and serene posture shows that he remains the eternal witness even while performing all of these acts simultaneously. Another great text of Kashmir Shaivism, the Pratyabhijñahrdayam, states that as human beings, we perform these five acts every moment and it is only because of our ignorance and delusion, that we are not fully aware of this power. Gaining the awareness that we do indeed initiate the same five acts as Shiva does, allows the mind to rise to the state of pure consciousness and attain union with Shiva.

Ganges ~ ("the one who goes swiftly") The most sacred river of the Hindus that flows east through northern India. Revered throughout India, it is worshipped in its personified form as the goddess Ganga. Pilgrimages to its holy waters are done in the belief that bathing in it brings about the forgiveness of sins and helps one attain salvation. Dying close to it or having your cremated ashes scattered in it are considered extremely auspicious.

Gaya ~ One of the seven sacred cities in Bihar, India and a place of pilgrimage.

Gita ~ ("song") Usually refers to a sacred text. Guru Gita - Song of the Guru, describes the Guru/disciple relationship, the nature of the Guru as a force of awakening, and how to meditate upon him.

Gunas ~ ("strand, thread or quality") The three

basic qualities or attributes of nature which underlie all manifestation: sattva, rajas and tamas. All manifest creation is made up of a combination of these three gunas. Sattva is ruled by Vishnu, is of the nature of integration, and is characterized as white. It is the highest frequency and is buoyant with light. Sattva is knowledge, happiness, integration and infinite existence without differentiation. Rajas is ruled by Brahma and characterized as red. The nature of rajas is cyclic revolution – passion, churning and violent spinning – that which is spinning towards the center and that which is spinning out into infinite expansion. Tamas is ruled by Shiva. It is characterized as the abysmal, infinite black. It is a quality that is so dense that it is thought of as a black hole. Nothing emerges from it. It is absolute, dense, infinite blackness, with no light emerging and all qualities crushed into a compression so deep that nothing can be discerned. It is the origin of creation. To say that the Guru is beyond the three gunas means that he is the source of creation even before creation itself came into manifestation.

Gurubhava ~ (from the Sanskrit root bhuu ="to exist, to become") The expression or attitude of becoming one with, or becoming absorbed in the

Guru. Being totally immersed in the Guru, or identified with him. In many sacred texts, this concept is referred to as "becoming of equal taste" with the Guru. One of Baba Muktananda's favorite meditation practices involved the identification of each part of his body, mind and spirit with his Guru, Bhagawan Nityananda, and in this way he experienced Gurubhava to the fullest.

Guru Yoga ~ The basis of the Guru Gita. View the 108 verses together as a whole to understand this profound concept of achieving enlightenment through the relationship developed between the Guru and the devotee. (see margena)

Hamsa ~ (see SoHam)

Hari ~ another name for Vishnu. (see Vishnu)

Hatha ~ (from the Sanskrit roots ha = "sun/solar"; tha = "moon/lunar") Balance between the sun and the moon. This symbolically means the connection of the soul to the body. Hatha Yoga is the third limb of the eight limbs of yoga as expounded by the great sage Patanjali, and involves physical postures designed to prepare the body for sitting for meditation and to enliven kundalini. Yoga means yoke or union and is used in the context of uniting the individual soul with the universal soul to achieve unity consciousness.

Imputed Terms ~ To attribute a quality to something. The ocean of consciousness that is referred to in the Guru Gita is beyond all qualities. Notice that even when you call something holy or sacred, it sets up a relationship with other things. If something is holy, there must be something that is more holy or less holy, and on and on it goes. To say something is beyond imputed terms is to understand that there is nothing to compare it to, nothing to match it up against. It also means that it is the same for everyone who experiences it. Normally when we experience something, we each have a unique perception of it. For example, smelling a rose brings up different impressions for each person and an entirely different impression for a honeybee. This is not the case with that which is beyond imputed terms. Thus, that which is beyond imputed terms is referred to as empty, devoid of all relative qualities.

Ishvara ~ (from the Sanskrit root ish = "to rule") The Supreme Lord. The Eternal One. All that humanity can know of God, both transcendent and immanent. The fourth tattva, supreme divinity. (see tattva)

Jñana ~ (from the Sanskrit root jña - "to know, to experience, to learn") Spiritual sacred knowledge and the highest form of wisdom beyond dualistic thought. Transcendent knowledge of the Absolute.

Kailas ~ ("crystalline") A sacred mountain in the Himalayas, thought to be the abode of Lord Shiva, where Parvati begins her discourse with Shiva on the Guru Gita. As well as giving a setting for this discourse, it symbolizes the Guru Gita as coming from the highest, most lofty authority. It is also symbolic of this teaching being secret knowledge, coming from a rarefied, pure and difficult to access place. It speaks to this being part of the "Whisper Tradition," where, through oral transmission, the highest knowledge was bestowed.

Kala ~ An aspect of Shakti and the manifestation of the world.

Karma ~ ("action") The universal law of cause and effect governing the cycle of birth, death and rebirth. The concept that the accumulated effect of every action performed, whether good or bad, comes back to impact a person's destiny, lifetime after lifetime.

Kashmir Shaivism ~ An 8th or 9th century philosophy of non-dualism, espoused by Kashmiri sages, that recognizes the entire creation as the manifestation of Shiva, a singular, divine consciousness, or chitti. Followers of Kashmir Shaivism believe that all of Creation is divine. The philosophy considers everything to be a part of the ongoing creative activity of pure infinite consciousness. It explains how the unmanifest supreme can manifest as the universe. The central texts include the Shiva Sutras, the Pratyabhijñahrdayam, the Spanda Karikas, the Vijñana Bhairava and the Kularnava Tantra; and it could be said that the Guru Gita is also part of this tradition.

Kundalini ~ ("coiled one") The primordial Shakti lies dormant, coiled like a serpent, three and a half times at the base of the spine in the muladhara chakra. Once this mystical energy or life force is awakened, it then ignites the quest for spiritual knowledge in the seeker. Through shaktipat, a Siddha master is able to activate this divine cosmic energy so that it can arise and expand consciousness through the purification that it brings about.

Lotus ~ A plant from the water lily family that grows in muddy waters and produces majestic pure blossoms. Therefore it is thought to be a symbol of the recognition of pure consciousness emerging from the mire of illusion. The term lotus is also used as an honorific as in "bowing to a Guru's lotus feet", which is one of the ways that a devotee shows great respect for his teacher. The word lotus is also used to represent the chakras or energy centers in the subtle body, in that each chakra has a certain number of petals, like a flower. As the chakras are enlivened through spiritual training, their petals literally open like a lotus flower.

Mahasamadhi ~ (maha = "powerful, noble"; samadhi = "the great union") This symbolizes a state of consciously leaving one's physical body at death. It is also a celebration of the anniversary of such a passing. Baba Muktananda's solar mahasamadhi is October 2nd, 1982.

Mahavakya ~ (maha = "great"; vakya = "saying") Our English word "vocal" comes from the Sanskrit root "vak". These are the great sayings that most clearly express reality and are self-born proclamations arising from realization. They are known as the crest jewels of the Vedas and are: "I

Am That" from the Chandogya Upanishad of the Saama Veda; "Consciousness is Brahman" from the Aitareya Upanishad of the Rig Veda; "I Am Brahman" from the Brihadaaranyaka Upanishad of the Yajur Veda; and "The Self is Brahman" from the Chandogya Upanishad of the Saama Veda. (see Veda)

Mandala ~ ("circle" or "center") Symbolizes the wholeness of creation.

Mantra ~ ("from the Sanskrit root man = "to think") A series of sacred syllables or divine sounds that form a word or phrase that can be repeated during meditation or at any time to experience transformation. These syllables and sounds are saturated with the power to protect, transform and purify anyone who consistently repeats them. When a mantra is transmitted to a devotee from his enlightened Master, it is filled with Shakti and the intention of the Master, and is then said to be "chaitanya" or enlivened.

Margena ~ (from the Sanskrit root maarg "to seek, to strive") Means the way or the path and is used here in conjunction with Guru, as in Guru margena, to denote the path of the Guru. The path of the Guru really has two meanings: One – the instructions given by the Guru for the specific practices of spiritual training that he recommends. Two – the connotation that Guru Yoga itself is the swiftest road to realization. In verse 2 of the Guru Gita, Parvati asks Shiva, "kena margena" – which path shall I take to awaken?

Maya ~ (from the Sanskrit root maa = "to limit, to give form") The power of obscuration or the veil of illusion that makes it seem as though the world is separate from absolute consciousness, which ultimately is seen to not be true. Maya emerges as the sixth tattva, and is actually the divisive limiting power of the Divine, which is built into creation to bring mind and matter into being. It is the filter through which the infinite becomes finite and the formless takes form.

Muktananda ~ (mukta = "freedom" and ananda = "bliss") Baba Muktananda was a Shiva Guru from the Siddha lineage in India. He was a perfected master who was instructed by his guru, Bhagawan Nityananda, to come to America in the early 70's and introduce devotees to meditation through the gift of shaktipat (see shaktipat). Mark Griffin is part of the Siddha lineage and was a student of Baba Muktananda's.

Mukti ~ ("liberation") A release from the bondage

of birth, death, and rebirth. Same as moksha, freedom from the awareness of duality. Also referred to as enlightenment.

Nada ~ ("sound") The spontaneous inner sounds that connect the spirit with its origin. The mystic vibrations of the eternal. The primal sound from which all creation has emanated. The celestial sounds that are heard in higher states of meditation.

Neti Neti ~ (na = "not"; iti = thus) Literally translates as 'not this, not this', and carries the larger implication that there are no qualities or terms that may be imputed or attributed to absolute reality. (see imputed terms)

Nityananda ~ (nitya = "eternal" and ananda = "bliss") Bhagawan Nityananda is a revered saint from India who was the Guru of Baba Muktananda from Ganeshpuri, India. Nityananda was an Avadhut, meaning that he was a fully enlightened being from birth. He took mahasamadhi in 1961.

Pada ~ ("foot") In Hindu tradition, the feet of the Guru, both the literal feet of the outer Guru and the subtle spiritual feet of the inner Guru, are considered to be very sacred and are worshipped with great devotion.

Parvati ~ The powerful Goddess and second consort of the Lord Shiva. Mother of Ganesha, the elephant God, she is the representation of spiritual beauty. She is considered to be Shakti. The spiritual significance of Shiva's consort is the idea of the union of Shiva and Shakti. This refers to the dawn of full realization or enlightenment when Shakti, in the form of kundalini, rises from her position at the base of the spine and moves up through the sushumna, the central channel, awakening all the chakras and merging with the principle of Shiva at the crown of the head in the sahasrar.

Pinda ~ ("body") Kundalini shakti, the attainment of shaktipat – a pivotal event in the arc of a person's many incarnations. (see Kundalini/Shaktipat)

Pranam ~ Bowing with reference. Greeting with respect. Prostrating, lying in a reverentially prone position before a great being.

Pranayama ~ (prana = "the life force or the vital energy that sustains the body"; yama = "control") The fourth limb of the eight limbs of yoga as expounded by the great sage Patanjali that refers to disciplined yogic breathing exercises. Yama also means death, and in this sense it carries the connotation of bringing the breath to a standstill at the still point in the space between each breath. It is in this silence that awareness of pure consciousness can be realized.

Prasad ~ A sacred offering or a blessed or divine gift given by the Guru. The bestowal of grace or divine help. Anything that the Guru blesses carries his shakti or divine energy, and a disciple is then able to partake of this energy through this offering.

Prayag ~ ("place of sacrifice") A city in the north Indian state of Uttar Pradesh located at the confluence of the three holy rivers: Ganges, Yamuna and the invisible river, Sarasvati. It is believed to be the place where Brahma offered his first sacrifice after creating the world. The term "the three rivers" also symbolizes ida, pingala and sushumna, the three most important nadis or currents of the subtle body.

Puranas ~ ("belonging to ancient times") There are eighteen major Puranas that originate from the sacred scriptural texts ascribed to the compiler Vyasa. They are supplements to the Vedas. They contain stories of the incarnations of God and the history of the Universe from creation to destruction, as well as the instructions of various deities. The Guru Gita was originally 352 verses and recorded in the text of the Shri Skanda Purana. Skanda means a group or aggregate.

Rupa ~ ("form") The bindu, the enduring vision of the Blue Pearl that is the true form of the Universe. (see Blue Pearl).

Rupatita ~ Beyond rupa, known as niranjanam; merging with pure Being.

Sadashiva ~ (sada = "ever, eternally") Sadashiva is the term for Supreme Being, the eternal Lord Shiva. In Kaishmir Shaivite philosphy, the third tattva is Sadashiva, the level where Shiva has begun to stir and come into relationship with the universe.

Sadguru ~ (from the Sanskrit root sad or sat = "truth and purity") Means "true Guru" or divine Master. The great Master or perfect Guru is one who knows the way to liberation through personal experience.

Sadhana ~ (from the Sanskrit root saadh = "to go straight to the goal") Spiritual practices or disciplines designed to lead to enlightenment.

Sadhu ~ A spiritual seeker in search of liberation. Any

person who is practicing sadhana. The Guru Gita points out that a genuine sadhu is a servant and disciple of his Guru.

Sahasrar ~ ("thousand") The thousand-petaled spiritual chakra at the crown of the head. This seventh chakra is the gateway to the highest states of consciousness and is considered to be the abode of Shiva.

Samadhi ~ (from the Sanskrit root sam = "completely together"; and dhaa = "to hold") To hold completely together, as in one-pointed concentration or absorption. The eighth and final limb of yoga as expounded by the great sage Patanjali. The union of oneness and the highest state of super-consciousness, which occurs through the full awakening and unfoldment of the kundalini shakti. There are four states of samadhi: laya samadhi, savikalpa samadhi, nirvikalpa samadhi and sahaj samadhi.

Samsara ~ ("continual movement") The cyclic existence of reincarnation: birth, death and rebirth or transmigration. This word points to the idea of being stuck in the relative ever-changing aspect of creation without experience of the absolute non-changing reality. The conditioned endless karmic cycle of worldly existence that is transcended once one achieves the highest state of enlightenment. (see The Wheel of Cyclic Existence)

Saraswati ~ (from the Sanskrit saras = "flowing" and vati = "having") The Goddess of speech, learning, music and wisdom who also bestows knowledge of the fine arts and all that is refined.

Sattva ~ (see gunas)

Satyam ~ (sat = "real, pure, true") Universal truth. That which exists and is real, beyond illusion.

Seva ~ Selfless service, the desire to offer service for a greater cause without expecting recognition or acknowledgment.

Shakti ~ ("energy" or "power") Often referred to as the Goddess Shakti, the consort of Shiva. The second tattva, it is the life giving force, the potency of the female energy, the creative principle and its expression. Through training with a true Guru, one's spiritual energy or shakti builds up or accumulates, gradually empowering the seeker with the ability to realize the truth. Daily recitation of the Guru Gita builds up a storehouse of shakti.

Shaktipat ~ (shakti = "energy" and pat = "descent

or falling down") The transmission or descent of grace from a Guru to his disciple through touch, sight, sacred word or thought. Shaktipat activates the dormant kundalini in a person who is open to receiving it. This transference of energy from the Guru to the disciple is known as the bestowal of grace. Shaktipat is a gift given by the Guru.

Shiva ~ ("good or auspicious") The ruling force in our contemporary (or current) world system; the dominant law and the primordial Guru. The God of creation, regeneration and rejuvenation as well as destruction and annihilation, Shiva is often represented sitting on a tiger skin, holding a trident with snakes coiled around his neck and arms. He is shown sitting in meditation with his third eye open, hence the reference in the Guru Gita to Shiva with his three eyes. There are two aspects to Shiva: the Shiva who is transcendent and pervades everything, known as para-Shiva; and the Shiva who is immanent and exists in this world – the apara-Shiva. It is the para-Shiva, the transcendent Shiva, who is the author of the five acts. In order to perform the first three of these acts, he expresses himself as Brahma, Vishnu and the apara-Shiva. Brahma is responsible for the creative impulse; Vishnu is responsible for sustaining creation; and Shiva is responsible for destruction, bringing each phase of creation to a close. Kashmir Shaivism holds Shiva to be the pre-eminent God of all Gods. In his capacity as supreme Godhead, Shiva is recognized as the author of the Guru Gita. Mark Griffin is in the Siddha Lineage, which is a Shiva lineage that has its roots in the mystical tradition of Kashmir Shaivism. The Guru Gita springs from this tradition as well.

Shri ~ (from the Sanskrit root shri = "to flame, diffuse light") A term of respect or endearment that encompasses auspiciousness, grace, holiness, beauty and the sacred, all in one word.

Siddha ~ ("one who is accomplished") A perfected being who has realized embodied liberation. One who has attained the state of uninterrupted unity-consciousness and has perfect and permanent identity with the Source of all. Baba Muktananda and Bhagawan Nityananda are examples of Siddhas.

Siddhi ~ ("accomplishment") This refers to the highest accomplishment, which is the attainment of liberation. It is also sometimes used to refer to specific paranormal powers, which are the natural by-products of complete realization.

These siddhis include astral travel, clairvoyance, invisibility, levitation, the power of attraction, the power to realize one's every desire, knowledge of the cosmos, the ability to expand, possessing the strength of an elephant, the ability to manifest one's will, knowledge of the organization of the body, omniscience, as well as many others.

Smritis ~ (from the Sanskrit root smr = "to remember") That which is remembered. A body of religious scriptures composed after the Vedic period, around 500 BC.

SoHam ~ (So = "That"; Ham = "I") A mantra that comes from the natural sound of the inhalation and exhalation of the breath. Thus with each breath the reality is stated "That Am I" – "I am Pure Consciousness". SoHam is equivalent to the mantra Hamsa, "I Am That". The use of the mantra SoHam or Hamsa is known as 'ajapa japa'. Japa means the repetition of a mantra. When 'a' is placed before a Sanskrit word, it creates the opposite meaning. So ajapa means non-repeating. In other words, this is the mantra that is repeated without doing the practice of repetition, because it is naturally being done for us by the breath itself. SO has its root at the first chakra at the base of the spine, while HAM has its root at the crown of the head at the sahasrar. SO represents all of manifest creation, while HAM represents the ocean of pure consciousness.

Tattva ~ ("principle") There are three uses of this word in the Guru Gita. One: Its first use is Guru Tattva. Here it means the principle of the Guru, and points to the idea that the Guru is more than just a person; it is also a universal concept – a force of awakening. Two: There are also references in the Guru Gita to the thirty-six tattvas. This concept originating from Kashmir Shaivism, states that all of reality can be viewed as thirty-six levels of different principles. The progression of tattvas continues from most abstract and subtle to progressively more manifest principles of creation. The first and most subtle layer is the principle known as Shiva, representing pure transcendence without any object. The second principle is Shakti and represents the first stirring of manifestation. The third tattva is Sadashiva, the level where Shiva has begun to stir and come into relationship with the universe. The fourth tattva is Ishvara, and is a level of supreme divinity. The fifth tattva is shudda vidya, which is pure knowledge. Maya is the sixth tattva and generates the next five tattvas, known as the five kanchukas ("jackets"), which are mixed values of purity and impurity. They represent omnipotence and a sense of limited power (kalaa); omniscience and a sense of limited knowledge (vidyaa); perfection and a sense of limitation of desire (raaga); eternity and a sense of limitation based on time (kaala); and omnipresence and a sense of limitation of space (niyati). The next five tattvas are the individual soul (purusha), the basic matter of the universe composed of the three gunas (prakriti), and the aspects of mind: the intellect (buddhi), the ego (ahamkara) and the mind itself (manas). The next five tattvas are the sense organs: the ears, skin, eyes, tongue and nose. The next five are the organs of action: speech, locomotion, sexual organs, organs of excretion, etc. The next five are the essence of what is experienced by the senses: sound, touch, form, taste and smell. The last five tattvas are the five elements of the material world: ether, air, fire, water and earth. When the Guru Gita speaks of the thirty-six tattvas as a garland for the Guru, it is understood to mean that the Guru is the Lord of the principles of all manifest and unmanifest reality. Three: Lastly, the Guru Gita refers to the Guru as the 'prime tattva': the Guru as the first or highest principle, Shiva himself.

GLOSSARY OF SELECTED WORDS 146

Tree of Life ~ An ancient mystical concept used in cultures throughout the world symbolic of knowledge, ascension, the cycle of life and eternity. With its branches reaching up and its roots reaching down, the tree of life symbolizes the link between the three worlds: heaven, earth and the underworld. It is that which unites them all. It is also often shown as an inverted tree superimposed on the figure of the human body, with its root system in the sahasrar and the space over the crown of the head, and the branches spreading throughout the nadis of the subtle body of the human form.

Vajra ~ ("thunder" or "diamond") Thought of as a thunderbolt, the weapon of Indra represents adamantine strength. In Tibetan and Buddhist culture the vajra, the "diamond" scepter, is used by deities as a ritual tool and represents the Bodhicitta, the mind of enlightenment. (see Bodhicitta)

Varanasi ~ the modern name for the Indian city of Benares, or as it was historically known, Kashi, one of the Wonders of the World. This is Shiva's city, one of the most holy cities in India, and is sacred to both Hinduism and Buddhism. It is said that Shiva dove into the world in the Himalayas, and resurfaced, like a diver coming up for air, in Kashi. Varanasi is said to be over 12,000 years old, with a population living there on the banks of the Ganges throughout that time period, making it the oldest continually inhabited city on earth. Varanasi itself is considered a gateway to liberation, in that many believe that simply dying in Shiva's city is powerful enough to break the cycle of rebirth.

Vedanta ~ ("end of the Vedas") A principal branch of Hindu philosophy that originated from Vedic oral traditions and scriptures and focuses on moksha, liberation. They are the core teachings of the holy texts, the Upanishads, which are commentaries on the Vedas and are devoted to the nature of God.

Vedas ~ ("knowledge, wisdom") The oldest sacred scriptures of Hinduism comprised of four ancient texts - Rigveda (the original work, which are the hymns of wisdom), followed by Yajurveda (sacrificial rites), Samaveda (hymns and music) and Artharvaveda (rituals designed to counteract disease and other specific practical applications). The whole body of them are known as 'Sruti', "what was heard". The Vedas are believed to have been directly cognized by the ancient seers, who spoke of the fundamental truths of reality, which they recognized while in the highest states of samadhi. The Vedas represent the mystic teachings, beliefs, hymns and prayers of the ancient sages, the Indo-Aryans of Northern India.

Vijñana ~ (from the Sanskrit root vi = "apart"; jñaa = "to know") Insight, discrimination, cognition, wisdom – the ability to distinguish the real from the unreal.

Vishnu ~ ("to pervade") Vishnu is one of the Gods of the Hindu triad with Brahma (the Creator) and Shiva (the Destroyer). He is known as the preserver and maintainer of the Universe. He is thought of as a manifestation of the One Supreme God. His wife is the Goddess Lakshmi. He is frequently depicted with four arms holding a discus, mace, conch shell and lotus. He holds a discus in his upper right hand, which represents the purified mandala of the universal mind. He holds a mace in his lower left hand, symbolizing the life force. He holds a conch shell in his upper left hand, the symbol of creation. He holds a lotus flower in his lower right hand, representing purity, liberation and perfection. It is Vishnu who descends from time to time to take incarnation as an avatar to restore dharma or righteousness. Some of the incarnations of Vishnu include: Rama, Krishna, the Buddha, Jesus, Zoroaster and Meher Baba.

Wheel of Cyclic Existence ~ The Twelve Spokes of Dependent Origin which describe the journey from birth through death to rebirth. The cycle goes from ignorance > dispositions > consciousness > name and form > six sense fields > contact > feeling > desire > appropriation > becoming > rebirth > aging and dying. Ignorance results from believing you are the body and knowing only the three states of relative consciousness: waking, dreaming and deep sleep, with complete ignorance of the fourth state of consciousness, the transcendental ocean of consciousness. This ignorance gives rise to the condition of dispositions, which is interdependent cause and compound effect. This in turn gives rise to consciousness, which is a sense of singular identity and the beginning of the ego. As identity is formed, we then see the development of name and form, which represents a separation of "I" and "That" and we begin to define ourselves as separate perceivers. This perception occurs through the development of the six sense fields (sight, sound, taste, touch, smell and intuition). With the development of the six sense fields, we then begin to reach out and touch the universe. This is the quality of contact. As soon as contact is generated, it gives rise to a condition of feeling and this produces a psychic imprint of sensation. These in turn lead to desire or grasping. Having experienced something, we try to hold on to it. This gives rise to the condition of appropriation, which is the process of saying, "This is my experience". It is attachment. The cumulative effect of all this emotion, desire and grasping, leads to a large collection of "baggage", which we have become and are now identified with. The fruit of this mass of identity consciousness seeks a form dedicated to repeating those experiences again and again, and thus we have rebirth. As soon as we are born, we immediately begin aging, decaying and dying. We experience this death as suffering, but the Wheel of Cyclic Existence shows us that it is really just a result of one condition having led to the next condition, which leads to the next condition, and so on. The intervention of the Guru allows this cycle to be broken at any number of spokes of this wheel, which frees us from the cyclic nature of samsara.

Other Books by Mark Griffin

108 Discourses on Awakening

The Bardo Thodol ~ A Golden Opportunity

Samadhi Kunda

Six Session Vajra Guru Yoga

Spiritual Power (2009)

Kundalini (2009)

Emptiness (2009)

Wheel of Cyclic Existence (2009)

108 Discourses ~ Volume 2 (2009)

~ Jewels ~
Selected Talks from the 2007 & 2008
Weekly Meetings (2009)

These titles and more are available
through our Online Store:
visit www.hardlight.org/store/

Audiobooks by Mark Griffin

Everything and Nothing
India Yatra 2008
Kali and the Guru
Kundalini - 1
Kundalini - 2
Kundalini - 3
Love Is An Act Of Will
MahaShivaratri
Power
Prana Apana
Prana, SoHam, 4 Bodies
Rupa ~ The Blue Pearl
Samadhi Kunda
The Awakener
The Bardo Thodol
The Chöd
The Focal Point Of Intention
The Guru-Disciple Relationship
The Mechanics of Shaktipat
The Perfection of Wisdom
The Recognition of Consciousness
The Six Session Vajra Guru Yoga
The Thread of Continuousness
The Universe
The Wheel of Cyclic Existence
The Grace Waves of Guru Yoga
Varanasi 2008
What Is Here Is Everywhere
What Is Shaktipat?
Zen And The Art Of Cessation, Observation And Samadhi

Guided Meditations by Mark Griffin

Bodhicitta I
Bodhicitta II
Bodhicitta III
Divine Will
Kundalini
Listening To The SoHam
Pranayama
Pratyahara I - Distilled
Pratyahara I - The Five Stages
Pratyahara II
The Awakener
The Breath
The Space Between The Breaths
The Union Of Shiva And Shakti
Tune In To The Guru Radar

These titles and more are available
through our Online Store:
visit www.hardlight.org/store/

www.ingramcontent.com/pod-product-compliance
Lightning Source LLC
LaVergne TN
LVHW041957060526
838200LV00018B/372/J